Digital Disruption in Australia

A GUIDE FOR ENTREPRENEURS,
INVESTORS AND CORPORATES

Nick Abrahams

Digital Disruption in Australia / Nick Abrahams. —1st ed.
ISBN 978-0-9942515-2-7

Table of Contents

1. How to Use this Book 3

2. Summary of the Disruption & Tech Deal Activity in

   Australia 2012-2015 5

3. Key Issues to Consider in Tech M&A Deals 25

4. Detailed Analysis of Tech, Media & Telco Deals in

   Australia 2012-2014 31

5. Key Contacts in the Australian Tech Sector 71

6. List of Australian Tech, Media & Telco Deals 2012-

   2015 85

7. About the Author 158

8. Stay Up-to-date with Disruption & Special Offers... 161

9. Index 163

Everything changes, nothing remains without change.

BUDDHA

or put another way

Everyone has a plan 'till they get punched in the mouth.

MIKE TYSON

Thanks

I am grateful for the remarkable support of many people in getting this book and relevant newspaper articles done.

Thanks to all the partners & staff of Norton Rose Fulbright, including specifically: Lita Tropea, Christine Kilzi, Daniel Johnson, Warwick Andersen, Jim Lennon, Jacqueline Masterman, Mary Keating, Jennifer Saines, Daniel Healey, Murray Whiteford, Robert Symons, Greg Vickery, Roger FitzSimons, Alison Chong, Alex Boxsell, Angela Johannson, Ju Young Lee (former employee), Aurora-Marina Lee, Caroline Waldron, Richard Lewis, Adrian Ahern and Wayne Spanner.

I would like to thank the tech journalists and editors at the *Australian Financial Review, Sydney Morning Herald* and *The Age*, including specifically Paul Smith, Ben Grubb, Lia Timson, Stephen Hutcheon and Asher Moses.

Thanks also to those people in the TMT sector whom I have had the pleasure of working with over the years (many of whom are listed in chapter 5) and special thanks to Phil Morle, Michael Firmin and Danny Gilligan for their help with reviewing some of the content and Michael Alf for helping publish this book.

All profits from the sale of this book will be donated to Alzheimer's Australia in memory of Audrey Abrahams.

To Simone, Oscar, Felix and Louis
  Thank you for your patience, love and support!
Love Nick/Dad

1

How to Use this Book

This book seeks to show the impact of digital disruption in Australia by reference to the deals that have been done in the Australian technology, media & telecommunications (**TMT**) market from 2012 to 2015. This has been a period of unprecedented corporate activity in the TMT market, driven largely by digital disruption. This book is intended to be a reference source for anyone seeking to understand more about what deals have happened, popular trends and where the future opportunity is in the Australian TMT market.

The structure of the book is as follows:

Chapter 2: Summary of Disruption and Tech Deal Activity in Australia – This is a summary of the major drivers of disruption and deal activity in the Australian TMT market during the years 2012 to 2015.

Chapter 3: Key Issues to Consider in Tech M&A deals – This is the only vaguely legal aspect of the book. It sets out some of the unique aspects of TMT transactions. It is critical to keep these in mind when negotiating TMT deals.

Chapter 4: Detailed Analysis of TMT Deals in Australia 2012-2014 – This is a republication of several articles I have written for, variously, the *Australian Financial Review, Sydney Morning Herald* and *The*

Age. These articles detail the key transactions in the TMT sector for each year during 2012-2014. They also go into detail in relation to some of the major trends, such as the interest of US venture capitalists in Australian tech companies and the recent boom in tech IPOs and backdoor listings.

Chapter 5: Key Contacts in the Australian Tech Sector – This is a list of some people and organisations who can help out with starting, growing, funding and selling TMT companies in Australia. There are lists of Corporate Advisors, Accountants, Recruitment Agencies, Accelerators, Incubators, Venture Capital Funds and PR Agencies. There are many people who I am sure I have missed putting on this list, and to those I extend my deepest apologies and ask them to contact me so I can include them in the next edition.

Chapter 6: List of Australian TMT Deals 2012-2015 – This is a detailed list of (close to) all the TMT M&A/Investment deals in Australia for the years 2012 to 2015. I may have missed some and, if I have, my apologies. Please feel free to send me details for inclusion in the next edition and my regular mailing list updates. Please note that the information about the deals is taken from public sources (newspaper, internet reports, etc.) and may not be accurate. This is especially the case with the stated transaction values

CHAPTER 2

Summary of the Disruption & Tech Deal Activity in Australia 2012-2015

The Dot-com boom/bust at the turn of the century was a harbinger of amazing things to come. The internet had promised so much, but had not delivered and shame fell upon those who had promoted the pipedream. Such was the animosity post-crash, I felt it more socially acceptable to return to being a lawyer rather than continue being an internet executive.

Some Australian internet companies survived and have become household names – SEEK, Realestate.com.au and CarSales. But, mostly, they went by the wayside or their ASX-listed carcasses were back-doored into mining companies to ride the resources boom for the next decade. It was to be years before a tech IPO was to happen again on the ASX.

How things have changed! Since 2012, tech in Australia has truly boomed. We have seen unprecedented levels of investment, corporate activity and value creation arising from the sector.

Why the change?

Disruption.

Traditional business models have been and are being massively disrupted by technology. Industries have been destroyed (remember encyclopaedias?), major companies wiped out (RIP Kodak) and value chains completely broken (think digital music or newspapers). Navman had great market positioning in consumer GPS until Google and Apple turned their attention to maps. WeightWatchers has seen its share price slide over 80% in four years as people turn to wearables like Fitbit and online health programmes like Australian success story 12Week Body Transformation.

All companies are being forced to embrace technology or face the consequences. No area of human endeavour is immune. The timing and scale of the disruption may differ from industry to industry, but all will be impacted.

Australia is a global leader in digital disruption – so we need to buckle up and enjoy the ride. According to the 2015 Harvey Nash Global CIO Survey, 56% of Australian CIOs reported their companies have been affected by digital disruption, which is 21% higher than the global average. A PricewaterhouseCoopers report warned that 5.1 million Australian jobs were at risk as a result of the impact of digital disruption. Even accountants are not safe, with the report finding that almost 100% of the tasks done by accountants today will be automated by 2035.

David Thodey, recently retired CEO of Telstra, says of his 40 years in the ever-dynamic telecommunications industry that the greatest rate of change has been in the last two years.

Catherine Livingstone, President of the Business Council of Australia, gave a landmark speech on disruption at the National Press Club in April 2015. She stated that, in the US, 40% of the workforce works freelance via new models like Airtasker, Airbnb and Uber, noting that the last two companies, while market leaders in their sectors, don't even own hotel rooms or taxis.

Disruption tips for companies

1. Alliancing: Focus on being good at working with other organisations in order to create a great customer experience. This includes the very significant challenge of co-opetition, working constructively with your competitors to bring services to market jointly.

2. Talent: Great people are going to be key to keeping up with the speed of change. Each demographic of employee will be important, and their respective needs/motivations are different. HR policies will need to be flexible to accommodate. Hats off to Telstra, which is trialling "Design your own job" and "Choose your own boss" programmes. I look forward to "Write your own paycheque".

3. Get lean: Most organisations do not respond well to failed projects. The whole concept of lean innovation is to de-stigmatise failure. "Fail fast" and learn, but don't blame the team. Equally, crack the nut on how to reward people who take chances and innovate.

4. Culture: Corporate values are critical - give people a higher purpose.

This global backdrop of ferocious change has driven the current boom in the Australian tech scene. Startups are moving quickly to maturity and in some cases global leadership. The movement is not slowing down. If anything, the speed is faster and the opportunities getting bigger.

Here is a summary of the key trends that have been occurring in the Australian tech sector over the last few years:

1. *M&A/Investment Mania:* In the last three years, there have been over 500 M&A/investment deals in the technology, media and tele-communications sectors. The transaction activity has been getting progressively greater each year. Clear trends are emerging as to which types of companies achieve successful investment rounds and ultimate exits.

For more detail on the M&A/investment trends, see the various articles summarising deal trends each year contained in Chapter 4. For a (very close to) complete list of all TMT-related M&A/investment deals in Australia since 2012, see Chapter 6.

In summary, some of the key trends have been:

- Media companies were big buyers of consumer-focused online transactional businesses. They have mostly sold these interests down now and are focussed on filling gaps in their content portfolio. The reported $45M paid for KidSpot and the $30M paid for Alan Kohler's Business Spectator Group show what remarkable valuations can be achieved via buy-side competitive tension.

- Australian companies have been successful building global cloud businesses that solve a problem for small-medium businesses at a low price point, think Invoice2Go and Campaign Monitor.

- Telcos are consolidating as it will be important to have scale once NBN comes on stream fully. This creates opportunities for smaller, nimble players to enter the market.

- Advertising-related technologies are of great interest at present. Some companies in the adtech space have listed recently and have re-markable valuations. Look out for companies with capabilities in programmatic trading of ad spots, mobile advertising and data analytics.

- Marketplaces like HiPages, Airtasker, ServiceSeeking, Freelancer and OneFlare have been popular investments recently and seem to be growing very well. Look out for fragmentation opportunities as new entrants move from broader offerings to specific offerings. This trend is referred to in the US as the "unbundling of Craigslist," where marketplace startups carve out niches from Caigslist. Over there, it has attracted US $9 billion in investment so far. Some niche marketplace examples in Australia include TidyMe (home cleaning), Expert360 (consulting) and LawPath (legal services).

- Developing a local version of a successful model from the US or other markets works well with attracting local investors. Seeing the model work at scale overseas de-risks (to a degree) the investment. The dream result is that the foreign giant will come and buy the local business, such as happened when MenuLog was bought by global player Just Eat for 371 times EBITDA. Happy days.

- FinTech is a very hot market right at the moment. See detailed comments below.

- Telstra are a big buyer of/investor in Australian tech companies. See detailed comments below.

Disruption tips for investors

1. Integrity: Look for investees with high integrity. Likely, the business you are investing in will pivot a number of times before it becomes successful. You want people who are going to be open and honest with you, their team and their customers. Can't go forward always watching your back.

2. Domain expertise: It is hard to disrupt a business-model unless you have a deep understanding of how that model works. There are many ideas which seem to the outsider to be great and likely to succeed, but usually only a true insider who can identify an opportunity and execute on the disruption.

3. Follow-on: Depending on the phase in the company's capital raising and growth, it is likely you will be asked to make additional investments further down the track. Make sure you budget for those further raises so as to avoid dilution.

4. Portfolio: As nice as it would be, chances are some of the investments are going to fail; therefore, look to establish a portfolio of smaller investments, not a big bang.

2. Multiples – *All over the place:* Valuation is a critical issue when it comes to investing in or divesting fast growth companies. In the early days (seed or angel investments), agreeing to a valuation is extremely hard. Generally, the company is pre-revenue and sometimes pre-product – so there are no metrics to base a valuation on. As a rule of thumb, think about giving 20%-30% of the company to the investors at each round. But, it varies massively. The key consideration is to ensure that the founder(s) are left with sufficient equity that (even after dilution in later rounds) they will still have a meaningful shareholding, which will act as an incentive to keep them building a great business.

The golden rule with valuations is that investors and potential company buyers are persuaded by the valuations of comparable companies. Therefore, the best way to justify a particular valuation is to point to valuations for comparable companies. The easiest source of these are the valuations of similar companies listed on the ASX. The investee is then valued at a discount to the market comparison based on its relative maturity.

It becomes difficult if there are no or limited directly comparable companies on the ASX. The easiest alternative approach is a discounted cash flow valuation. However, given the idiosyncratic attributes of the tech market, DCF may not be appropriate. I will now do something very dangerous and give some indications of valuation multiples. I say dangerous as, while this is not on the same level as say BASE jumping, it is dangerous because people will all have very different views about these metrics.

Here are some thoughts:

Scenario A: Company making EBITDA

If the company is growing very fast and looks set to continue that growth, the valuation of the company may be 8 to 10 times annual

EBITDA (historical or maybe forward projections) or even considerably more.

If the company is growing reasonably fast, but growth looks like it is slowing to a degree, the multiple may be 5 to 8 times annual EBITDA (historical or maybe forward projections).

If the company has reasonably low growth (say 5% or less pa), then the multiple may be 3 to 5 times annual EBITDA (historical) or even less.

Scenario B: Company making revenue but not EBITDA

This is very hard and really depends on numerous factors, including growth rate and time to break-even if that is the strategy. However, it should be noted that break-even may not be a goal for the company. For example, if the business is like Amazon where Jeff Bezos is doing a "land-grab" and is not interested in EBITDA, the investor needs to look at the longer term prospects for the company.

While it varies widely, there is some precedent for fast growth, no-EBITDA, cloud business to be valued at 10+ times projected annual revenues.

Before people send me notes about how wrong these numbers are, can I just say that these numbers are a very rough guide. At the end of the day, the valuation is whatever the parties (with their own unique circumstances) choose to value the company at. If a company desperately wants to buy the business and can see a significant "synergy value" to the acquisition, it may choose to pay well over the odds for the business.

3. The Lean Mantra: During the Dot-com Bubble, entrepreneurs built the businesses they believed customers needed without really talking to the customers pre-launch. Now, the customer is critical to the development process. No longer do you "build it and they will come." Rather, "lean methodology" is about getting your product into market as soon as possible, the so-called "minimum viable product." Feedback from customers dictates product development, the idea being that most ideas and product innovations will fail, so it is better to fail fast and cheap rather than slow and expensive.

4. CloudSpeed: It is possible to grow companies much faster and with less money today due to the cloud. During the Dot-com Bubble, startups had to spend money on hardware and services to get basic infrastructure to set up websites. Today, cloud providers like Amazon Web Services make this infrastructure available on demand and at a bare fraction of the price it used to cost.

Australia's fastest ever startup to exit story is the Spreets group - buying rocketship. Spreets went from whiteboard startup to $40M sale to Yahoo!7 in just over 12 months.

> **Disruption tips for entrepreneurs**
>
> *1. Just do it: Don't just think about it, get the "minimum viable product" into market as soon as you can.*
>
> *2. The rapier not the broadsword: Make sure you have a very clearly defined product and market. Investors are wary of entrepreneurs who believe they can solve multiple problems.*
>
> *3. Team: It is trite, but every successful person says "surround yourself with smart people." You do not need to always be the smartest person in the room.*
>
> *4. Motivation: Work to change the world for the better – don't just do it for the money. You are more likely to get some change and it will be more rewarding anyway. Keep all the balls in the air – it's not all work. Look after your health, family, friends and spirituality. Counter-intuitively, I have seen many entrepreneurs go into depression as they struggle for life-meaning after successfully selling their business. On a positive note, they do seem to come out pretty quickly – and not just because they bought a big boat.*

5. *Location, Location, Location – Not:* Australian businesses have always suffered from the "tyranny of distance." If you wanted to do business overseas, it required very significant investment in offshore sales and support personnel, or sub-optimal partnering arrangements.

Because of the viral nature of the internet and power of search engine marketing/optimisation, it is possible to expand into global markets without leaving home. Chris Strode, founder of Invoice2Go, built his app to 100,000 customers globally (and $100M in value) from the central coast north of Newcastle. Email marketing powerhouse, Campaign Monitor, received a $250M investment from Insight Venture Partners valuing the business at $600M, without leaving the Cronulla area.

For more information on this topic see "The $1 Billion Love Affair with Aussie Tech" at Chapter 4.

6. *US Venture Capital Loves Us:* The US VCs have well and truly found Australian tech companies. It all started back in 2010 when Accel Partners invested $60M in Atlassian. Today, Atlassian is a global software heavyweight valued at billions of dollars – an amazing investment return for Accel.

Since then, the rest of our tech community has experienced the Atlassian halo. There are several US VCs who are in Australia every couple of months scanning the market for fast growth tech companies. Together, they have invested over $1 billion in companies in Australia in the last three years.

These days, they are prepared to invest in Australian "Pty Limited" companies and do not necessarily require the company's structure and leadership to be "flipped up" to the US. However, it is important to note that they are looking to invest $20M-$30M for 30% of the company, so the business needs to be at scale already if you want to attract the big US VCs.

For more information on this topic see "The $1 Billion Love Affair with Aussie Tech" at Chapter 4. For a list of US Venture Capitalists with interests in Australian companies, see Chapter 5.

7. Our Tech Venture Capital Community is Back: Many of the Australian tech-focussed venture funds suffered poor returns in the years following the Dot-com Bubble. This led to the drying up of tech VC funds generally. This trend has been reversed in recent years with many new funds popping up. The Atlassian team and others have put significant money into the Blackbird fund, while SEEK founder, Paul Bassat, and colleagues have set up Square Peg. Daniel Petre and Craig Blair are hoping to repeat the success of their Nettus days with AirTree Ventures and Michelle Deaker is investing broadly in the sector via One Ventures.

For a list of Australian venture capital funds, see Chapter 5.

The angel investment community has also grown remarkably over the last few years. For a list of Australian angel investment organisations, see Chapter 5.

8. Thank Mining for all the ASX Risk Capital: With the downturn in commodity prices, the Australian mining sector has taken a big hit. This has meant that Australian high risk capital, which normally sits in the more speculative of the ASX-listed mining/exploration companies, is now looking for a new home. This flight of capital was the catalyst for 40 IPOs and backdoor listings of tech stocks on the ASX in 2014, compared with five in 2013. The ASX is giving boom-time valuations to fast growth tech stocks at present.

For more information on this topic see "Record Numbers Queuing up for Back Door Listings" at Chapter 4.

9. Australia's Tech Ecosystem Comes of Age: Australia is starting to achieve a critical mass around the tech ecosystem. There is now a large variety of co-working spaces, incubators and accelerators to help early stage companies grow. In addition, there are numerous tech-focused service providers such as corporate advisers (who help companies to raise money and do M&A), accountants, lawyers, PR agencies and employment agencies.

For a list of co-working spaces, incubators, accelerators, corporate advisers, accountants, lawyers, PR, and employment agencies, see Chapter 5.

10. The Government Listens & Helps: It is understood at the highest levels of government that a vibrant start-up/tech community is critical for Australian competitiveness and productivity. The Abbott Government has recognised this with:

- changes to the tax treatment of employee share/option schemes to encourage companies to give employees equity participation;

- largely leaving the research & development tax incentive untouched. This incentive is one of the most effective means of the Government supporting early stage companies;

- promising to facilitate crowd funding, though it may be 2016 before we see this come to fruition;

- replacing Commercialisation Australia with the Accelerating Commercialisation grants programme;

- granting the small business tax incentives in the 2015 Budget; and

- requiring "Significant Investor Visa" migrants to invest at least $500K of the $5M they are required to invest in Australia into an Australian venture capital fund.

Certainly, the Government could do more to promote investment in fast growth tech companies. Governments around the world are setting policies to foster dynamic innovation ecosystems. A stand out is the United Kingdom, where start-up investors can get up to 50% income tax relief.

Even China is focussed on the opportunities. Premier Li recently announced China's "Internet Plus" initiative. This seeks to mandate that traditional industries, like healthcare and manufacturing, must proactively embrace digital disruption.

11. *We can do FinTech:* Most start-ups these days seek to have a global customer base from day one as our market is too small. Our financial services sector is an exception. It is big enough to get a FinTech business to significant scale without the need to go offshore. In addition, FinTech is by nature geo-specific because of the need to comply with local regulations. This creates great opportunity as the financial services sector will be significantly impacted by disruption.

Surveys of attitudes towards banks show that younger generations are very comfortable getting financial services from Apple and Google rather than the existing banks.

The payments market is the first major battleground for the big banks. Long-time local disruptor Tyro has made its mark already. However, it is players like Google Wallet and Apple Pay which pose the biggest threat.

The loan market may also come under threat with innovations such as peer-to-peer lending. A 2015 Morgan Stanley report says the Australian P2P lending market will hit $20 billion by 2020. This is good news for the likes of Society One and Ratesetter who are getting traction.

Even deposit-taking is not safe with Chinese colossus, Alibaba, recently raising $120M in deposits from 200 million new accounts.

Of all the new FinTech challenges, nothing has the potential to disrupt like cryptocurrencies. Bitcoin is the most famous of these, but similar block chain technologies like Ripple are fast making inroads. Commonwealth Bank recently announced it was using Ripple to transfer payments between subsidiaries.

The regulators are watching. ASIC Chairman, Greg Medcraft, has gone on record to say that ASIC is monitoring digital disruption in the financial services sector very carefully, especially the impact it may have on the cyber-resilience of organisations. It is a fine line for legislators and regulators. Over-regulation will stymie innovation and enhance the power of the incumbents who are able to absorb the costs of compliance. Under-regulation leads to risk in the system.

In early 2015, a group of passionate executives from financial services corporates joined with some VCs, KPMG and the NSW Government to establish Australia's first FinTech innovation hub, Stone & Chalk.

12. Corporate Venturing in Vogue: Until recently, very few companies had corporate venturing divisions. However, many have now followed the likes of Intel Capital into this complicated space. Westpac has invested in a $50M FinTech fund called Reinventure. Optus has Innov8, AMP has AMP Ventures, ANZ has Innovyz, Wesfarmers has its Emerging Ventures unit, and Telstra has its Ventures unit for larger synergistic investments and successful early-stage accelerator muru-D. KPMG has joined with Artesian Venture Partners to create an alliance to better facilitate corporate venturing.

13. Telstra: My advice to budding entrepreneurs is to build a company Telstra wants to buy. Telstra is, by far, the most prolific acquirer of tech businesses in Australia. Under David Thodey's leadership, Telstra has made major moves in the Australian eHealth space and have made significant smart investments into US companies Docusign, Box and Oyala.

14. *Forget the Law – Focus on the UX:* Companies have grown strong businesses by ignoring some legal issues and focusing on great user experiences. Google copying text from a website to show in their organic search results is arguably a breach of that website's copyright. But, the website wants to be listed in Google's search results, forget the breach of copyright. In the early days, YouTube had a lot of content on its site without relevant licences, but has now signed licences with the world's major content owners who want the access to YouTube's audience. Similarly, Airbnb and Uber have had allegations that their services breach local laws following them as they expand around the world. However, regulators recognise the value of the sharing economy to their communities, so have displayed some flexibility and preparedness to innovate.

15. *Corporate Karma:* At the core of many successful tech companies is a strong desire to change the world for the better. This is certainly a key driver in Silicon Valley as can be seen with Google's "Don't Be Evil" motto and ground-breaking employee-friendly working conditions. This has been reflected in Australia with Atlassian, whose core values include "Play, As a Team" and "Be the Change You Seek." However, most resonance comes from their reworking of the old favourite: "The customer is always right" which, translated into Atlassian-speak, is the value: "Don't fuck the customer." Hard to argue with that honesty.

Predictions:

It wouldn't be a discussion about disruption if I didn't offer some thoughts as to the future:

1. **ASX will fall out of love with tech:** The current rosy valuations for pre-profit and, in some cases, pre-revenue fast growth

tech stocks will fall away as businesses fail to live up to expectations. The first door to close will be back-door listings, then IPOs. My advice would be to move fast if you think a capital raising via the ASX is for you. If you do list, make sure you raise enough money to get to cash flow breakeven. If the market turns, it will be hard for a pre-profit tech company to raise additional capital.

Anatomy of a disruptor: LawPath.com

This example sets out some of the key elements investors look for in a disruptor.

1. Problem that needs fixing: *Legal services are expensive and not easy to acquire efficiently.*

2. Massive potential market: *Current Australian legal market is $21 Billion pa. and global market is more than $900 Billion pa.*

3. Simple pitch: *LawPath uses cloud technology to make legal easier and affordable. Think Xero for Law.*

4. Clear Product Offering: *Customers can get a discounted, fixed price quote on any legal matter from the 600+ network of LawPath lawyers within 4 hours. Also, if businesses subscribe, for $49/month, LawPath CloudLegal subscribers get:*

> *a. unlimited 30 minute calls to LawPath's 600+ network of lawyers;*

> *b. unlimited access to 200+ legal/commercial documents; and*

> *c. ability to store their completed legal documents in their own MyLawPath cloud account.*

5. Traction: *LawPath has had over 10,000 customers since starting two years ago.*

Note: The author's family company group hold shares in LawPath.

---

2. **China is critical:** China has a developing venture capital industry and Australian tech companies will benefit. The recent

Australian Government requirement for Significant Investor Visa applicants to invest $500,000 into Australian venture capital funds will help as 90% of the 800 Significant Investor Visas issued so far have been issued to Chinese people. Australian fast growth company Airtasker recently raised $6.5M, much of it from China, while Telstra's accelerator, muru-D, has been very successfully taking its graduating startups to China to secure follow-on investment.

3. **User experience designers will become like gods:** Currently Data Engineers are in huge demand and this will continue as big data becomes a critical part of all organisations. However, user experience will also become key. In the words of Steve Jobs, "Simple can be harder than complex."

Companies are looking for more seamless/magic-like experiences for their customers. Apps are critical. In 2014, Apple paid more to app developers than Hollywood movies took at the box office. Expedia and eBay get, respectively, 90% and 60% of their revenue from apps.

Such will be the importance of UX designers, that people like England-born Apple design guru, Jony Ive, will get knighthoods (okay so that has already happened, but maybe even more designers will get knighthoods).

4. **Social Media – Boom!:** Social is massive already, but it will become even more pervasive. The "word-of-mouth" power of social media will impact traditional advertising as advertisers seek out social influencers. Content marketing will get bigger and more searching will be done within social media apps. Messaging apps like Kik, WeChat and WhatsApp will become powerful social media players in their own right.

5. **Retail's wild ride continues:** According to a Harris Poll in the US, 46% of American's *showroomed* (looked at product in-store

but bought it online) compared to 69% who *webroomed* (looked at online but bought in-store). The linkage between the online and the offline retail presence seems critical and "*omnichannel*" is the mantra.

Great lessons to be learnt from Nordstrom Rack's integration of offline and online presence for purchases and returns. Pure-play online retailers will need an offline presence, so look out for Amazon buying a big traditional retailer sometime in the next few years.

6. **Disruptors get disrupted:** It feels like the only constant from now will be disruption. Look at how hotel booking disruptors like Wotif have themselves been disrupted by Airbnb. Indeed, 16-year-old Google is in the process of being disrupted by 8-year-old iPhone as, according to a survey by Flurry, people spend 80% of their smartphone/tablet time inside apps and only 20% on the mobile web.

7. **Disruption in schools:** Clayton Christensen's seminal text on disruption "The Innovator's Dilemma" and its sequel "The Innovator's Solution" will become compulsory reading in business studies classes at high schools. Uber's disruptor is likely currently in year 9 being taught the importance of debits and credits. The traditional school commerce education needs to be expanded to include entrepreneurship and disruption.

8. **Cyber security will get worse before it gets better:** Currently, cyber risk is among the top three risks for most organisations. Hacks are a daily occurrence. This will continue to get worse. One alternative is for organisations to move to private networks rather than using the public internet infrastructure, but this would severely impact the economics and growth of the digital economy. Technical solutions will need to be found,

but the forecast for the medium term does not look promising.

9. **Privacy will be a marketing battleground:** Large corporates already have enormous amounts of information about us. The genie is out of the bottle – it will not go back in. We will be prepared to trade our personal information for value/services (Gmail scanning is only the beginning). However, we will be attracted to those organisations that respect our privacy. Success will come to those companies that provide us with a great service because they know so much about us – not those who overstep the mark and spam us.

   The world will follow the European Union and people will demand the "right to be forgotten".

10. **Block chain everything:** We have only scratched the surface of what is possible with block chain, the tech at the core of all cryptocurrencies like Bitcoin. The decentralised public ledger of transactions has enormous opportunities for all manner of business interactions.

11. **Net neutrality will struggle:** The telcos, as owners of the big pipes which make the internet happen, are unlikely to sit idly by as the over-the-top providers like Netflix and others make fortunes off their assets. It is possible that there may be different classes of internet traffic – a bit like a repeat of the air mail/sea mail pricing differential in the offline world.

12. **MOOCs again:** Massive Open Online Courses will completely change the economics of universities as the physical presence of students becomes less relevant. Prestigious institutions like Harvard have been quick to embrace the MOOC phenomenon.

   I need to be careful here. I went on record some years ago as saying that virtual world's like *Second Life* would completely change tertiary education. Shortly after my pronouncement, the US Government cracked down on the sex and gambling in *Second Life* and it sank like a stone. Oops, got that wrong.

13. **Generation Z picks up the phone:** The millennials (born in the 1980's and early 90's) have been a tough nut for marketeers to crack with their need for authenticity in the message. Generation Z (born after 1995) are smarter, more confident and way more connected than any generation before them. They are also the first generation to be born mobile. They will never really know a desk top computer.

14. **Everything else:** Just to make sure I can say I got at least one prediction right, keep your eye on telco consolidation, Internet of Things, Big Data, the Sharing Economy, Virtual & Augmented Reality, Drone-enabled logistics, Crowd-funding, Everything-As-A-Service, Everything-Over-The-Top and Wearables.

Finally, if you believe the conspiracy theorists, if all goes according to plan, at some stage in the next 50 years, the machines will have achieved their goal of "Singularity" - the point where artificial intelligence exceeds human intelligence and we work for them. I look forward to the irony of computers calling helpdesks because their human doesn't work properly.

The Conclusion

What is the legacy of all this disruption for the world and our children? According to Catherine Livingstone, the jobs of 47% of the US workforce are at risk due to artificial intelligence. The PwC report I mentioned earlier says the safest professions are doctors, teachers and advertising/PR people. It would be an unusual world if these were the only four jobs you could choose from. Both PwC and Livingstone agree that lawyers will become completely disrupted. Who knows, maybe it will end up being more socially acceptable for me to say I am an internet executive than a lawyer.

Critically for Australia to be a successful, innovation-rich economy, there needs to be a cultural shift. We love the middle too much. We don't like the tall poppies and we distrust bankrupts. To prosper in this new world we need to celebrate the successful and offer encouragement to those who have failed such that they may succeed on their next try. Now, that is a bold and exciting future for Australia!

CHAPTER 3

Key Issues to Consider in Tech M&A Deals

The purpose of this chapter is to provide a high level overview of some of the key issues arising in connection with an M&A deal that has a strong IP/IT focus.

As with any transaction, it is important from the outset to undertake detailed due diligence investigations on the target's corporate profile, its assets, and its major contractual undertakings. In particular, when dealing with a target with a key IP/IT portfolio, it is necessary to review the IP/IT assets and all agreements the target has entered into relating to those assets.

The following sections touch on some due diligence points and structural issues that prospective buyers/advisers need to be mindful of when dealing with IP/IT matters.

Ownership of IP

Confirmation should be obtained from a target that it either owns, or has valid enforceable rights to use, all IP and IT that is used in its business. The process of confirming ownership of IP can be done in a number of ways, but most practically by:

1. Searching relevant registers – governmental or otherwise (such as trademark or patent registers or registers for ownership of domain names);
2. Reviewing all documents relating to the ownership of IP and any third-party agreements pursuant to which IP rights are granted to the target; and
3. Interviewing relevant stakeholders.

From a transactional structuring perspective, it is also helpful to obtain detailed warranties around the ownership and use of IP/IT rights. What also follows from this is that it is necessary to ensure that the IP/IT owned and used by the target is all that is required to operate its business.

Depending on the nature of a particular transaction, if the core IP/IT is owned outside of the target group (and ownership of IP/IT (rather than rights to use) are a fundamental requirement), transitional arrangements may need to be put in place to ensure that IP/IT is transferred into the target group.

IP Infringement

Broadly speaking, there are two core areas of concern to a buyer when acquiring an IP/IT portfolio; these are:

1. Infringement by the target company of a third party's intellectual property rights. IP infringement litigation is very costly (particularly patent infringement litigation) and can take years to resolve. Consequentially, it is essential to understand what the key infringement risks are up front and make all necessary enquiries to determine whether the target will be restricted from operating without fear of infringement suits.
2. Infringement of the target company's intellectual property by third parties. Knowing whether the target company is aware of third-party infringement is useful in determining the value

of the target company's intellectual property assets. Such infringement suits (or prospective suits) should be reviewed and considered in the due diligence process.

Contractual Rights

A thorough due diligence includes a review of material agreements to which the target is a party, and significant from an IP/IT perspective are licensing arrangements. It is also worth noting that licenses can appear in a range of agreements that are not necessarily identified as such – for instance, under research and development contracts, joint venture arrangements, consulting distribution and software development agreements.

For agreements where the target receives a license to use a third party's IP/IT, the buyer should confirm that the scope of the license is broad enough to cover all current and anticipated future uses of the licensed IP/IT (including the right to make modifications, if applicable) and contains ownership provisions allocating ownership of any permitted modifications.

For agreements where the target company grants a license to a third party to use the target company's IP/IT, the buyer should confirm that the scope of the license is narrow enough to ensure that only those rights needed by the licensee are granted, the target's ownership of its IP and/or IT is clearly stated, and the licensee is obligated to maintain the confidentiality of the target company's intellectual property and technology.

Other key points to look out for in license arrangements include: the parties, definitions and description of the IP/IT involved, exclusivity and non-compete obligations, field of use, relevant royalties, term, warranties and indemnities, governing law and jurisdiction, and any specific provisions that could impact on the proposed transaction (such as change of control and assignment provisions).

Source Code

Possession of the source code (which is, in its simplest form, intellectual property in the form of copyright) is usually critical to the target's ability to operate its business platform or to evolve its products and services. Care needs to be taken to ensure that, if the target does not have possession of the source code, appropriate arrangements are in place to ensure the third-party provider is obligated to provide support to the target (and if required, its customers). The buyer should also confirm whether any source code for the target's products has been provided to any third party, whether to an escrow agent or directly to a third-party licensee.

Open Source Software

The manner in which open source software is used by a target, and the open source license governing its use, can have a significant impact on the target's IT arrangements. It is, therefore, critical to obtain a complete and accurate listing of all open source software used by the target and copies of all applicable licenses, and a description of how such open source software is used. Depending on the nature of those open source arrangements and the underlying product, the buyer may decide that it has other preferred open source software products it wishes to integrate with the target business.

Employee Issues

Generally speaking, in the absence of an agreement to the contrary, ownership of IP initially vests in the inventor. An exception is that in Australia, an employer automatically owns the copyright created by an employee. However most employment arrangements should contain an IP assignment provision. Therefore, the buyer should confirm that all of the target's employees and contractors have executed written agreements assigning ownership of all IP/IT developed by them during the provisions of services to the target. In certain limited circumstances, a license from the employee or contractor to the target company may be sufficient, though those cases should be carefully reviewed prior to a determination of sufficiency.

Non-Competes

Once a deal has been struck it is prudent to ensure that, to protect the value of the buyer's investment, appropriate non-compete obligations are entered into by relevant stakeholders. Fundamental to this is ensuring the restraint is enforceable on policy grounds (in other words, if someone is paid for the restraint, it is more likely to be upheld). For the target, the key is to ensure that, if there is potential to "trip" the non-compete, appropriate "carve outs" from the non-compete obligations are built into the transaction documents.

This was first published by the author in a Norton Rose Fulbright Legal Update.

The material in this chapter is owned by Norton Rose Fulbright and licensed to the author for the purposes of this book.

CHAPTER 4

Detailed Analysis of Tech, Media & Telco Deals in Australia 2012-2014

Article 1: Analysis of 2014 telco deals.......................... 32

Article 2. Analysis of 2014 tech deals.......................... 34

Article 3. Analysis of US venture capitalists Investing in Australian tech companies....................... 42

Article 4: Analysis of tech companies listing on the Australian Securities Exchange.................... 46

Article 5: Half year analysis of 2014 tech deals............ 51

Article 6: Analysis of 2013 tech & telco deals............. 57

Article 7: Analysis of relative merits of listing on ASX or in the US 61

Article 8: Analysis of 2012 tech & telco deals............. 64

Article 1: Analysis of 2014 telco deals

First published in the *Australian Financial Review* on 24 February 2015 as

Telco M&A Responds to NBN Landscape to Boost Revenue Streams

http://www.afr.com/technology/web/nbn/telco-ma-responds-to-nbn-landscape-to-boost-revenue-streams-20150223-13dpnr

The Australian telco sector is in the midst of big changes with the NBN coming on stream.

Australian telecommunications merger and acquisition deals last year were largely driven by an industry responding to the threats and opportunities posed by the NBN. The remainder of 2015 will likely see more consolidation in the sector as companies recognise that it is the scaled providers who will prosper in an NBN world.

Here is a look at last year's telco deals and what that can tell us about where the activity may be this year:

NBN Co: It is not every day an $11 billion deal gets signed, but Telstra and NBN Co have now done their deal twice, signing the new multi-technology-network-enabling contract in mid-December after almost a year of negotiations.

One of the negotiating team said to me: "I've done this contract twice now. I don't have another round in me." Hopefully too, for Australia, this is the final version.

Also announced late last year were the separate deals between NBN Co and Telstra and Optus, enabling the use of the HFC networks left stranded by the original NBN deal.

Telstra opens the purse: In an NBN world, Telstra will procure wholesale fixed services from NBN Co after progressively transferring ownership of Telstra's copper and HFC assets. Telstra's acquisitions in 2014 illustrate that Telstra is focused on customer experience and new revenue streams.

On the customer service side, Telstra invested in Mountain View-based MATRIXX Software, a company which provides customers with real-time data usage reports. The telco invested in Nexmo, a company that assists with communication to customers and Telstra also joined an investment round into US-based mobile phone authentication services provider, Telesign.

Asian expansion was clearly on the agenda with the acquisition of regional telco Pacnet for $858 million and Telstra is also making an important strategic investment in the Indonesian market via a joint venture with Telekom Indonesia.

Other revenue streams that Telstra invested in include three acquisitions in the eHealth space and a joint venture with Australia's largest home/business security monitoring company, SMP Security. Telstra Chief Executive, David Thodey, has been focused on the growth potential of its cloud computing business and bolstered it during the year with the $60 million (rumoured) acquisition of network integrator and advisory firm, O2 Networks.

Telco buys tech: Telcos need to get up the value chain from pure carriage provision and, consequently, many are looking to acquire IT services businesses.

ASX-listed broadband provider BigAir bought managed services provider Oriel Technologies for up to $15 million. Inabox Group bought IT and cloud services provider Annitel for $10 million, and iiNet bought 60% of Tech2 Group, a provider of professional technology services under various brands including Gizmo.

Datacentres heat up: Holder of some of the most secure federal government files, Canberra Data Centres received $140 million from Quadrant Private Equity for a 45% stake. While Vocus paid $11.7 million for ASG's Perth datacentre, Vocus continued its consolidation play buying EDC's data centre business earlier this month*.

The new contender: Vocus also made a well-received bid to acquire west coast telco, Amcom, for $635 million. This will create the nation's third largest provider of corporate telecommunications when the deal is expected to be approved in April.

ASX open for business: Hong Kong satellite services firm, Speedcast, had iiNet founder Michael Malone join the board and later in the year raised $150 million in an IPO on the ASX. Meanwhile, shopping centre Wi-Fi player SkyFii raised $3.5 million in a backdoor listing.

2015: The Australian telco sector is in the midst of big changes with the NBN coming on stream. Change creates opportunity and we should expect this year to see Telstra get even more aggressive in its onshore and offshore M&A strategy.

The junior telcos are likely to continue their consolidation as will data centre providers. IT services companies with a cloud focus can expect to see interest from the telcos as everyone seeks to enhance their revenue streams beyond carriage.

Article 2. Analysis of 2014 tech deals

First published in edited form in the *Australian Financial Review* on 3 Feb 2015 as

Disruption Juggernaut Will Drive Tech M&A in 2015

http://www.afr.com/technology/web/disruption-juggernaut-will-drive-tech-ma-in-2015-20150202-131650

Tech M&A was up 55% globally last year and the investment activity in Australian tech has eclipsed the heady days of 2000. It would appear that all those much maligned Dotcom v.1 entrepreneurs were right – the Internet does change everything! It just took 14 years, not 14 months.

In 2014, the stars truly aligned in the tech heavens with investment activity being driven by:

Disruption: Fear of tech-based disruption has boards imploring management to buy into innovation if they can't do it internally. The mantra is more Bitcoin and less Kodak.

ASX: With 40 tech companies coming onto the exchange in 2014, the mining collapse has caused the public market to open its arms to tech like never before.

US VC: US venture capitalists have discovered Australia (thanks Atlassian!) and see great value here.

AUS VC: In 2014, money flowed into (and out of) Australian venture capitalists like Square Peg, Blackbird, Airtree (got $60M), Reinventure (got $50M), Bailador (listed on ASX) & BlueChilli (got $5M),

Cloud: Cloud means Australian tech companies can participate in global markets from day one.

Scale: Thirst for scale drives consolidation, locally and globally.

Here is a summary of the key themes and selected deals of Australia's tech 2014 (see table for more info), followed by some predictions about where the shopping spree will continue in 2015.

Consumer Internet

The largest number of transactions was clearly in the consumer internet space.

Travel: Expedia grabbed Wotif for $700M, TripAdvisor picked up Sydney-founded online tour agency Viator for $200M, and Fairfax decided not to stay with vacation rental site Stayz and took $220M from US giant HomeAway. The huge costs of digital marketing and keeping pace with technological advances (mobility particularly) in the B2C space means these companies need global scale.

Property: REA (owners of realestate.com.au) bought an initial 17.2% stake in ASX-listed, Asian-focussed online property business iProperty for $106M, then increased its stake to 19.4% with the sale to iProperty of REA's Squarefoot business. Using some loose change found down the back of one of the office couches, REA also paid $15M for property rentals website 1Form. Meanwhile arch-rival, Domain Group (aka Fairfax Media) shelled $50M to pick up Canberra-focussed online property player, Allhomes.

Marketplaces: Ellerston Capital led a $6M round into successful home services marketplace HiPages. Similarly, local services marketplace Oneflare secured $1M from Equity Venture Partners and the Sydney Seed Fund. Shiftworker marketplace OneShift sold 27.5% for $5M to staffing management company Programmed. Pumped up from their $3.5M of funding in 2013, odd-jobs outsourcer Airtasker bought Taskbox and Melbourne site Occasional Butler. Freelancer acquired virtual content marketplace, Fantero. And marketplaces of sorts, RSVP and *Oasis, tied the knot to create the dominant online dating business in Australia.

Online gaming: Crown Resorts paid $10M for the 50% of Betfair it did not already own. UK gaming giant Ladbrokes, obviously pleased with its purchase of Brisbane-based Gaming Investments in 2013, doubled down paying $20M+ for Eskanders Betstar.

Financial Services

Australia has successfully developed many tech companies focused on the financial services sector, and 2014 was a good year to be in that zone as fears of disruption ran riot.

Payments: 2014 was the year that we finally understood "why so many taxi apps?" Uber and Australian contenders GoCatch and ingogo revealed taxi payments are just a beachhead through which to grow a much broader payments business. The idea clearly resonates, with Square Peg putting $4.5M into GoCatch and a group of high net worths putting $9M into ingogo. One can't help but feel that Cabcharge, with its legacy sole play taxi business, is a bit of a deer in the headlights of the disruption juggernaut.

APAC expansion led NYSE-listed Global Payments to pay $305M for Queensland-based integrated payments company, Ezidebit. Aussie payments network, Cuscal, now challenges the big banks after its acquisition of Strategic Payments Services from Bendigo & Adelaide Bank and MasterCard for $37M. The purchase will give Cuscal 10% of the electronic funds market in Australia. Listed UK identity intelligence specialist, GB Group, bought credit fraud detection company DecTech Solutions for $37M.

Lending: Carsales paid $60M for 50.1% of Australia's biggest car finance broker, *Stratton Finance, while Australia's largest financial software company, Rubik, had a big year with the acquisition of two mortgage industry software companies, Stargate Technologies for $20M+ and Infinitive for up to $17M. The two acquired companies account for almost a quarter of all broker-originated mortgage settlements.

Security

With major breaches like Sony Pictures and Target occurring almost every day, the money is pouring into IT security companies. UXC Consulting boosted its capabilities with the acquisition of cybersecurity services business Saltbrush Group. ASX-listed services provider PS&C paid $8.3M for white hat cybersecurity company Pure Hacking. China's Shenzhen Infinova acquired electronic security equipment provider, Swann Communications, for $85M.

Services Companies Seek Scale

In a consolidation play, Dimension Data paid $171M for local consultancy business, Oakton. Data#3 bought Brisbane-based IT consultancy, Business Aspect Group, for $6M and 42% of Wi-Fi analytics company, Discovery Technology, for $1.5M. Deloitte bought Canberra public sector consultancy, Analytics Group, for $6M. Deloitte has foreshadowed it will continue to make further acquisitions. RXP Services paid $5M for Hobart-based Microsoft consultancy Insight4.

Coming to Australia

NASDAQ-listed Cognizant acquired mobility and cloud provider Odecee and its 150 strong workforce. Another NASDAQer, SPS Commerce, paid $17M for Leadtec, our leading provider of cloud-based supply chain solutions. The French consulting company, Valtech, bought startup digital consultancy, Neon Stingray, to become its APAC headquarters. UK's Tribal Group paid $15M for student management systems player Human Edge.

US Venture Capital

Ever present on our shores these days, the US VCs had a very big year, with Insight Venture Partners leading a $250 million investment into quiet achiever, Campaign Monitor - one of the largest VC deals done anywhere in the world during the year.

Accel Partners, flush from its success with Atlassian, 99designs, and Ozforex, invested $35M into NSW Central Coast phenomenon *invoice2go. Insight Venture Partners gave the chequebook a nudge, with one of its investees, Unitrends, acquiring NICTA spinout and cloud integrator, Yuruware, for $10 million.

Facebook and Expedia investor, *Technology Crossover Ventures, made its first foray into the Australian market with a $30 million Series B investment into SiteMinder, a global force in online hotel booking. Sequoia Capital came with $12M to invest direct into LIFX, LED smartbulbs startup.

IT management solution provider, ScriptRock, received $8.3M from Square Peg and big US angels, Peter Thiel and Scott Petry. Shoes of Prey got $6M from a variety of Silicon Valley high net worths. Founders Fund put $3.6M into online design website, Canva. BugHerd got $1M from a consortium led by US-based 500 Startups.

Online video provider, Viocorp, got an injection from niche US funder Partners for Growth.

Telstra

The best advice to any budding Australian tech entrepreneur is build something Telstra wants. Flush with funds from NBN Co and a solid core business, Telstra was splashing the cash this year with the $1B share buyback and over 10 acquisitions/investments. Telstra Ventures participated in: a $19M Series B round with Asia-focused mobile advertising company, AdNear; a $58M pre-IPO round with Bigcommerce; a round in electronic signatures firm, Docusign, reportedly valuing it at $1.8B; and a direct investment into Australian cloud software company Panviva.

Telstra Health has been busy, acquiring positions in: cloud developer, Cloud9 software; radiology/pathology secure messaging service, MediNexus; health software developer, iCareHealth; and AUS/NZ dual-listed eHealth player, Orion Health Group. Given that Telstra has spent well over $100M on eHealth-related acquisitions, it has shown it is serious about its stated goal of being the market leader in eHealth in Australia. It will be fascinating to see Telstra weave these disparate assets together into a cohesive force, but if anyone can do it, Telstra has the capacity (and wallet) to do it.

ASX – IPO & Backdoor

The end of the mining boom freed up a lot of speculative capital in the listed space. The public markets have clearly forgiven the tech sector for its errant ways in Dotcom v1. In 2014, there was an unprecedented 19 tech IPOs and 21 tech backdoor listings. Many different types of tech businesses in various stages of development were listed. Some standout themes were cloud, e-commerce and software. One of the most interesting companies to backdoor was US-based 1-Page, which had very little connection to Australia other than an interest in accessing our capital markets. The stock came on at a 600% premium and has settled to around a 500% premium, making it the standout listing for the year. This warm reception will not go unnoticed in Silicon Valley with many VCs enquiring about the potential exit opportunities via the ASX.

Predictions

As I said at the beginning, the stars truly aligned for tech in 2014 and there is no reason to think things will change in 2015. Some specific thoughts:

Taxi melodrama: The taxi app wars will continue – maybe this year will see a shakeout of one of the main players?

Cloud-everything: There is no doubt the move to cloud is driving revenue pipelines in software and services businesses. Nimble, industry-focused cloud businesses will continue to be attractive to the major players.

Get on the exchange quick: The recent volatility on the ASX generally will likely lead to a less receptive atmosphere for tech IPOs/backdoors. Might be best to move in the first half of the year to ensure the door does not close. Some interesting companies have publicly mentioned a possible float this year: Wisetech, ingogo, MYOB, *Martin Jetpack, Future Fibre Technologies, InfoTrack, Costa Group, Touchcorp and AussieCommerce.

IT Security: Given the fallout from recent high profile hacks, this is the one area of IT that boards are very interested in at present. This will drive customer spend and, consequently, interest in larger security players acquiring high quality niche operators, especially as the technology in the intrusion detection space is moving so fast.

Private Equity: No doubt we will see more US venture capitalists invest in our fast growth tech businesses in 2015. However, I also think the established Australian private equity players may look to take positions in our more mature tech businesses. Tech has not been a sector where these investors have been particularly active previously, but I think the medium-term strength of the sector will make it too attractive for them to ignore.

Telstra: This year might see Telstra Health focus on consolidating its acquisitions while Telstra Ventures will continue to pick up positions in interesting companies here, Asia and the US.

Cryptocurrencies: I was an early crypto-sceptic but I, like many large financial organisations, now believe there is a genuine opportunity for cryptocurrencies to massively change the financial services sector. The mistake I think is to get too focused on Bitcoin. There are over

500 cryptocurrencies around and it may be that solutions like Ripple are better suited for adoption by the banks.

Disruption, disruption, disruption: It is happening everywhere. While you might not get replaced by a robot next year, be careful not to be too cocky about your five-year outlook. This disruption creates massive opportunities for entrepreneurs and corporate intra-pre-neurs, not to mention the solo-preneurs, mum-preneurs, wanna-pre-neurs and every other sort of preneur. My best wishes for an exciting 2015 to you all.

Article 3. Analysis of US venture capitalists Invest-ing in Australian tech companies

First published in the *Australian Financial Review* on 8 December 2014 as

The $1 Billion Love Affair with Aussie Tech

http://www.afr.com/business/banking-and-finance/private-eq-uity/the-1billion-love-affair-with-aussie-tech-20141208-122zou

The call started normally enough. "Hi, my name is Chris and I need a lawyer to help me sell my technology company." So far so good.

The next line caught me a little off guard. "I am on the Central Coast."

What tech companies are there on the Central Coast, I wondered. Little did I realise I was just about to hear one of the great Australian tech stories.

Chris Strode went on to describe Invoice2go. It sounded interest-ing, but I was still dubious about the scale of a business neither I nor hardly anyone in the Australian tech sector had ever heard of. I asked him who he thought would be interested in investing in the company. With his trademark casualness, he said a number of American venture capitalists had expressed interest but he had a term sheet from Accel Partners and thought they were the right fit.

I thought, "Accel. This is big – from the Central Coast and big!"

Over the past few years, the US VC community has pored over hundreds of Australian tech companies and have made more than 10 major investments, worth almost $1 billion.

Accel are the leaders of this wave, putting Australia on the map with their big plays into Atlassian, OzForex and 99designs. Their $35 million investment valued Strode's Invoice2go at more than $100 million, rivalling Erina Fair as one of the biggest businesses north of Newcastle.

Not bad for a guy who started the company with his wife, Michelle, nine years ago.

Atlassian has been the poster child for how a bootstrapped tech company can grow a global customer base from Australia. Accel found Atlassian because so many of their investees used the software that they invested in it, and a global tech superstar was born. It has been a sensational investment for Accel and its halo effect has brought many other US VCs to Australia's shores.

There are at least six US venture funds making regular trips here scouring our tech successes, such as Campaign Monitor ($266 million from Insight Venture Partners) and our unsung heroes like SiteMinder ($30 million from Technology Crossover Ventures).

Why Australia?

One US VC told me he loves Australian tech companies because, in Silicon Valley, entrepreneurs expect huge valuations based on little more than a fancy PowerPoint deck; but Australians can bootstrap ourselves to $10 million of earnings before interest and tax.

I did not think it necessary to disabuse him of this notion. While I am not sure we have a lot of companies that fall into this category because of the lack of early stage venture capital, our entrepreneurs are more likely to build businesses with prospects of early revenue than taking a "build it and they will come" approach.

It's hard to pay off a Sydney mortgage with "eyeballs."

The US experience with our entrepreneurs has been positive.

According to regular visitor to Australia, Alok Pandey of Vector Capital, "I have met many Australian technology entrepreneurs over the last few years and I am very impressed by their intelligence and work ethic."

The sheer weight of venture capital in Silicon Valley has caused valuation inflation in the US early stage tech world.

Simply put, US VCs can get better priced investments in Australia than at home.

Silicon Valley's emperor of early-stage investment, Dave McClure, says, "Australia has a lot of smart people, you speak English, and the prices are good."

He should know. McClure runs the incubator, 500 Startups, and has invested in over 20 Australian companies. He says his success rate with Australian investees is higher than his average.

It used to be that to break a business in a new territory you needed heavy marketing and physical presence. Not the case online – virality (or what we used to call "word of mouth") is the order of the day.

Invoice2go built a massive global customer base with almost no marketing – just a great application that people loved to use.

Campaign Monitor built a $600 million global business from Cronulla.

So, Australian tech companies can build global markets without the need to open offices (or even do marketing) overseas.

Betting on Australia

US venture capital

	Large deals (valued at over $10m)				Small deals (valued at or under $10m)		
Year	Target	Investor	Value ($m)	Year	Target	Investor	Value ($m)
2014	Atlassian	T Rowe Price	150	2014	Bugherd	Australian based Rand Stream Ventures & Starfish Ventures & US Based 500 Startups	1.0
2014	Invoice2Go*	Accel Partners	35				
2014	UPX	Sequoia Capital	12	2014	Canva	Shasta Ventures & Founders Fund	1.6
2014	Campaign Monitor	Insight Venture Partners	266	2014	Yoursmarr	Livetrends, Inc & Insight Venture Partners	13.0
2014	Siteminder*	Technology Crossover Ventures	30	2013	Bubble Gum Interactive	BHI Tal & various other investors	2.5
2013	Bigcommerce	Revolution Growth	40				
2012	Bigcommerce	Mike Maples & General Catalyst Partners	20	2013	App.io	Quest Venture Partners	1.0
2011	99designs	Accel Partners	35	2013	BuyReply	Valar Ventures, Square Peg Ventures & Adrian MacKenzie	1.0
2010	Atlassian	Accel Partners	60				
2010	OzForex Group	Accel Partners	70	2012	Happy Inspector	US investors	1.0

*Transactions arranged by the author and based on Yes No Rose Fulbright.

Australia: Easy-Access Asia

Until the past three years or so, all Silicon Valley venture capitalists wanted to talk about in the Asia region was China. However, the bloom has come off that rose.

Many VCs have discovered that China is a tough market to crack, business practices are not familiar and, frankly, China doesn't need their capital.

The VCs see Australia as an easy-to-access proxy for Asian growth. Pandey says "The Australian technology industry is ripe for significant growth in the years to come because of the talent and drive of Australian entrepreneurs and sheer size of the APAC market."

There is no doubt the success of Accel's Atlassian investment has attracted other venture capitalists and it has also given them comfort about deal risk. It used to be, if an American VC invested in an Australian company, the investment had to be made via a "flip-up" into a more familiar US structure like a Delaware corporation – an expensive and time-consuming effort.

These days, American VCs are generally happy to invest directly into Australian proprietary limited companies and are comfortable with our IP protection regime. They still regard our employee share options tax regime with incredulity; but, thankfully, the federal government is fixing that.

For the most part the big VCs want to go big. Their preferred cheque size is minimum $30 to $40 million for 20% to 30% of the company. One VC I spoke to reckons there are over 30 unlisted fast-growth Australian tech businesses which would command valuations in excess of $100 million.

Potential investees need to solve a problem for a global market. The VCs are not interested in Australia-only businesses. Their preference is for a proven track record with global expansion.

They are heavily focused on the big picture. They may well look for an investee which can be bolted on to one or more of their other investees to create a global powerhouse in the relevant vertical.

In the future, smart money, like the US venture community, will gravitate to successful businesses. Australian tech companies are getting more successful offshore and success will breed further success.

We can build great global businesses from our distant island.

To borrow from the old *New Yorker* cartoon with the dog in front of the computer:

"On the internet, nobody knows you're Australian."

Article 4: Analysis of tech companies listing on the Australian Securities Exchange

First published in the *Australian Financial Review* on 30 September 2014 as

Record Numbers Queuing Up for Backdoor Listings

http://www.afr.com/business/banking-and-finance/investment-banking/record-numbers-queuing-up-for-backdoor-listings-20140929-jl71k

Backdoor listings, or reverse takeovers, on the ASX look set to beat the record this year. It's a record, not surprisingly, set back at the peak of the dotcom boom in 2000 when 32 companies backdoor listed. For the first six months of this calendar year, there have been 16 backdoor listings – and there's fever in the market for taking tech stocks public this way. Based on current sentiment, 2014 will cut 2000's lunch well and truly. It is boom time for tech companies going onto the ASX.

There are so many tech companies being backdoored into mining stocks, Kalgoorlie's raucous annual mining conference may well need to change its name to "Diggers, Dealers & Developers."

Australian tech entrepreneurs have long complained that we lack growth capital. Sure, we have recently developed some good sources of early stage venture capital, but it has always been hard to find the $2 million to $5 million cheques. With the decline in the resources sector, the public markets have stepped in to fill this funding gap.

Contrary to popular opinion, there is a significant amount of risk-chasing growth capital in Australia. It has just been reserved for the listed junior miners and explorers. Once commodity prices go below a certain number, these speculative ventures become unviable. The choice is simple – give the money back to shareholders or find a new business to put into the shell. After having received the money, no self-respecting entrepreneur is giving the cash back, so the latter option is the preferred choice.

My recent weeks have been littered with meetings with either the owners of listed shell(s) looking for cloud businesses to put into the shells, or with bewildered tech entrepreneurs who have been approached by promoters offering "backdoors," "guaranteed shareholder spreads" and a fast track to liquidity.

I am not going to pass judgment on whether it is better to get onto the exchange by the back or the front door, to say nothing of whether these tech businesses are right for the costs and scrutiny of listing. Vocus and Village Roadshow are two very successful results of backdoor listing, so you never know. I will look at why shell shareholders like backdoor listing and what are the main reasons tech companies might look to be part of such an event.

Why Shells Like Backdoor Listings

Generally, the core business of these shells has become unviable, but they are sitting with $1 million to $2 million in the bank and sometimes, not always, they have been suspended from trading. If the shell acquires a tech business, then, while the existing shareholders might be diluted, they have at least some upside in the share price and, importantly, they are not restrained from selling their stock. The owners of the tech business that has been vended into the shell will generally be restricted from selling their shares for one to two years.

For investors, it is worth noting that, according to research by UTS's Peter Lam, most money is made on trading in the shares between the date the backdoor listing is announced and the date that the transaction completes. Interestingly, the shares are not required to be suspended from trading after the announcement, even though it is still possible that the transaction will not complete as it is subject to a vote by shareholders of the shell.

Backdoor Benefits

1. It is just an M&A deal: In this case, the shell and the target tech company are in the same or similar businesses, but the shell might be smaller than the target tech company, such as in the case when listed minnow, Mnemon, "acquired" the much larger Grays Online. Both companies were in e-commerce, so the deal made sense for Grays to get access to the ASX.

2. Idiosyncratic circumstances: In some cases, it may be that getting onto the ASX via the front door would take significant restructuring. For example, when Asian social media flyer Mig33 backdoored into Latin Gold, CEO Steven Goh said that, because the original business was a US/Singaporean hybrid, the business restructuring to get to an initial public offering would have caused significant delay and costs when compared to a backdoor listing

3. De-risk the listing: The process to backdoor list is transparent and direct. The tech company negotiates with the controller of the shell, a deal is then struck for the tech company to be acquired in return for a certain amount of stock. The rest is process and the tech target has the benefit of knowing that because the shell is listed already, it generally has (or can get relatively simply) the required spread (or minimum number) of shareholders holding minimum parcels. There is no significant risk associated with movement in the equity markets during the backdoor listing process.

By comparison, the IPO route has risk. The prospective company must engage advisers and seek to generate enough interest in the IPO to get to the required minimum number of shareholders. This may take several months and there are no guarantees. The arrangements could fall over at any stage up until listing, especially if there is adverse movement in the equity markets during the process.

4. Size matters: Generally speaking, underwriters like companies with a minimum of $10 million in revenue and annual growth rates of more than 30%. The alternative for smaller companies is to backdoor list. In addition to getting on the boards, the target company often combines the listing with a small ($3 million to $5 million) capital raise. It is often easier to raise the money this way as investors are attracted to the idea that there will be liquidity in the stock as a result of the listing (though such liquidity may not occur if the stock is ultimately thinly traded). The target tech company also gets the benefit of whatever cash the shell has in the bank, a handy start to the capital raise.

Backdoor Folklore

There is a general feeling that the backdoor listing process is simpler, faster and cheaper than an IPO. This is generally not the case.

1. Simpler than an IPO: There is a very similar process, whether the company is getting on the ASX by the front or the back door. For example, a prospectus/information memorandum is required in both cases. The only exemption to this requirement is where the shell and the target tech company have similar businesses that are of a similar scale such as in the Pie Networks and NewZulu listing. In these cases, a prospectus-like document is not required, making the process faster.

Adding to the complexity is that, in a backdoor listing, due diligence needs to be done on two companies (shell and target tech company) rather than just one in an IPO scenario. There will also be a sale agreement to be negotiated and likely a capital restructure.

2. Faster than an IPO: Because the process is similar, it is not necessarily true that a backdoor listing can get a company onto the ASX faster than an IPO. Indeed, because of the need to negotiate with the shell, it can take longer.

3. Cheaper than an IPO: The ASX costs are roughly the same, whether backdoor or IPO. One of the major costs of a backdoor listing or IPO is the need for a prospectus/information memorandum. So, unless the deal falls into the Pie/NewZulu category, a prospectus-like document and its attendant expenses will be required. The public markets are more eager to back tech companies than they have been since 2000 and, generally, the share prices of the companies coming to the market have performed well.

We need to hope that the market does not get flooded with the more speculative end of the tech world, as failure to achieve goals will be viewed harshly by shareholders, and a rash of poor performance has the potential to adversely impact the market for all tech stocks.

The last time we saw such a rush on tech companies coming onto the ASX was during dotcom. The resulting carnage tarnished tech stocks for many investors. Our regulators are a wake-up to the potential for trouble and, a few weeks ago, ASIC issued a warning in relation to the surge of backdoor listings. True, the fundamentals of tech businesses today are much better than they were back in dotcom, but there does seem to be a quote that is quite relevant for these times: "Those who fail to learn from history are doomed to repeat it."

Article 5: Half year analysis of 2014 tech deals

First published in the *Australian Financial Review* on 5 August 2014 as

Australian Tech Millionaire Production Line Gathers Pace

http://www.afr.com/business/banking-and-finance/investment-banking/australian-tech-millionaire-production-line-gathers-pace-20140804-j7121

I spent Saturday night as the odd man out surrounded by the young and beautiful. This was a crowd who would not be out of place at the Ivy or even the Logies. But no, it was The Australian Startup

Awards – a group of early-stage technology companies brought to fever pitch by uber-disruptor, Ruslan Kogan, who gave a rousing speech in favour of the pursuit of profits and success. They are right to be enthusiastic. The opportunity has never been bigger. The first half of this year has delivered great riches to Australian tech entrepreneurs. Here are the hot spots.

US Venture Capital Loves Us

Australian tech entrepreneurs used to shoot for a $20 million to $40 million exit and, after that, it was Byron Bay time. But the stakes have changed – Australia is growing tech companies to massive valuations in timespans as short as those seen in Silicon Valley. This has been spotted by US venture capitalists, and seven or eight of the main Silicon Valley VCs are on regular trips to Australia looking for the next Atlassian.

Insight Venture Partners led a $250 million investment into quiet achiever, Campaign Monitor. While the valuation was not officially released, it is rumoured to be about $US 600 million ($644 million).

This is one of the largest US VC deals of recent years anywhere in the world, only bested by funding rounds into Airbnb, Uber and Dropbox.

It was the first capital raise for the 10-year-old company and a great tribute to the founders, Ben Richardson and Dave Greiner,

Insight Venture Partners gave the chequebook another nudge, with one of its investees, Unitrends, acquiring NICTA spinout and cloud integrator, Yuruware, for $10 million.

Facebook and Expedia investor, Technology Crossover Ventures,* made its first foray into the Australian market with a $30 million Series B investment into SiteMinder, a global force in online hotel booking.

Online video provider, Viocorp, got an injection from niche US funder Partners for Growth.

PFG offers a novel form of debt/equity funding specifically for tech companies. It is unlike any funding available in Australia and they have completed a substantial number of transactions over here with relatively mature companies.

Other US deals are due to be announced in the not distant future.

What We Do Well in Australia

The internet has overthrown the tyranny of distance that kept Australia from being a global tech player.

Recent deals like Campaign Monitor and US giant Fleetmatic's acquisition of online field force management platform, Connect2Field* show Australia can build globally competitive companies that solve a problem for small and medium businesses at a low price point.

Look to the remarkable market cap of Xero – the Russell Crowe of the tech world. Born in NZ, matured in Australia, and now experiencing great success on the US stage.

The key thing US investors are looking for in Australian tech companies is an overseas customer base. Getting product/solution fit in Australia, then expanding to a global market is sure to raise the interest of major investors.

Online Consolidation

The internet is maturing and consolidation is rife. Sydney-based task-sourcing website Airtasker acquired Melbourne's Occasional Butler. Fairfax expanded its Domain business across Canberra and rural NSW by ponying up $50 million for All Homes.

When listed web host Melbourne IT bought up rival domain registry NetRegistry Group, $50 million was also the magic number

Love was in the air as Australia's two largest dating sites, Oasis Active* (part owned by the Ten Network) and RSVP hooked up in a $90 million merger.

APN, after its acquisition of brandsExclusive two years ago*, left the online fashion world by selling its stake in that company to IPO aspirant AussieCommerce, and Australian Associated Press left the media monitoring world with the well-timed sale of that business to iSentia.

The search for scale online is always important. Matt Barrie's Freelancer acquired Ukraine-based digital content marketplace fantero.com, an interesting geographic expansion at this time in Ukraine's history.

Financial Services – Always a Winner for Australia

Financial services is one of our strongest industries and is the focus of many online players.

Classifieds giant Carsales.com made a big move into the financial services sector by buying a 50.1% stake in online lender Stratton* for $60 million.

ASX-listed financial services firm Rubik acquired two mortgage brokering software companies, Stargate Information Systems for a reported $20 million upfront and Infinitive for $2.4 million. The two companies between them handle around 25% of all Australian broker-originated mortgage settlements.

Not keen to sit back and wait for the disruptors, Westpac, has shown it wants to get closer to them. Through its venture capital arm Reinventure, Westpac invested $5 million into Australia's first peer-to-peer lender, SocietyOne. They were joined in the investment by German internet powerhouse Rocket Internet and Justin Reizes, Australian head of KKR.

Telstra Continues to Be Active

Telstra had a big start to the year, selling 70% of Sensis to PE fund, Platinum Equity for $450 million, and using $50 million of spare change to joint venture in the monitored security industry with SNP, and $40 million for network integrator O2 Networks. Offshore, Telstra invested in US mobile phone authentication provider TeleSign.

Overseas Exits

There were some great exits to overseas companies. The world's largest travel site, TripAdvisor, paid $US 200 million for Sydney-founded online tour agency Viator.

But, British companies are also picking up Australian companies at a great rate. UK gambling giant, Ladbrokes, acquired Alan Eskander's Melbourne online bookmaker, Betstar, for something north of $20 million.

Tribal Group, a UK government-focused education support provider, acquired Human Edge Systems, an Aussie provider of student management systems for $15 million.

Not to be left out, GB Group, a UK-listed identity intelligence business, bought Australian fraud detector, DecTech, for $37 million.

Forget Mining – Get Into the Cloud

With the decline in the resources sector, we have seen numerous listed shells (and their ready-made register of shareholders) become available for backdoor listing. And the tech companies have really responded – feels just like old dotcom times.

Bulletproof Networks did a reverse takeover of mining company Spencer Resources. Macro Energy had been trading at 2¢ a share. It acquired bitcoin trading house digitalBTC, changed its name to Digital CC, and its stock shot up 42%.

Cloud financial planner, Decimal Networks, backdoored into mineral exploration company Aviva Corporation. Information security player, Cocoon Data, integrated with uranium explorer Prime Minerals.

Cloud applications builder, PRM Clouds, integrated with miner Minerals Corporation. Q&A social network, Spring.me, integrated with property player GRP Corporation. Cloud platform provider Cloud Central integrated with wine company Dromana Estate. PieNetworks bolstered its ASX standing with the acquisition of leading crowd-sourced journalism platform Newzulu.

Australian-founded mobile gaming company Mig33 got a $10 million investment from tech manufacturing giant Foxconn ahead of its integration with Mineral explorer Latin Gold.

However, one of the most remarkable deals is where Silicon Valley HR startup 1-page is doing a reverse takeover of ASX listed Inter-Met Resources.

1-page has no specific link to Australia, but is hoping to use the listing as a springboard to a NASDAQ listing. We may see more US start-ups coming to Australia to tap our capital markets.

The Next Six Months

We will continue to see strong tech M&A and investment activity, especially with US venture capitalists looking to invest in companies with a global customer base and enterprise value of $80 million plus. While the backdoor to the ASX will continue to swing, we may see more IPOs from the likes of Amaysim, Ingogo and Yatango. We also see IT services businesses searching for acquisitions to bolster their cloud capabilities. These businesses are struggling with the death of the five-year software replacement cycle as their customers move to "as-a-service" models.

Cloud businesses that solve a problem for SMBs at a low price point will continue to be attractive acquisition targets as a result.

Telstra will also continue to buy and invest, especially in healthcare and mobile-related high-tech out of Silicon Valley.

Elsewhere, media companies are more prepared to write cheques than they have been for a while.

For example, Nine just upped its investment in Quikflix by taking out HBO. Hopefully, this will continue.

The consolidation of online businesses will continue to occur, especially in the business to consumer space and financial services.

Further afield, the massive size and appetite for acquisitions of Chinese internet companies, like TenCent and Alibaba, means it can't be too long before we see them coming down here.

Article 6: Analysis of 2013 tech & telco deals

First published in the *Sydney Morning Herald/The Age* on 19 December 2013 as

2013: The Year Australian Tech Got Noticed

http://www.theage.com.au/it-pro/it-opinion/2013-the-year-australian-tech-got-noticed-20131218-hv688.html

Defying the downturn in general mergers and acquisitions, the Australian technology and telecommunications sector boiled over with more than 90 transactions of $1 million-plus this year.

Several trends were clear when we look back at those deals:

- In the telco sector, many companies jockeyed for a position in the post-NBN world.
- There was fall out and consolidation as the online retail juggernaut continued to surge, but not everyone got a ride.
- The rest of the world discovered Australian tech businesses and found them an economical way to fill a void in their product suites, while hunting for the next Atlassian.

- The Australian share market embraced tech stocks for the first time since dotcom – it appears all is forgiven, for the moment.

- Media companies lost interest in acquisition and quietly disposed of some non-performing assets. Telstra got its M&A mojo back and seems intent on buying anything involving a thermometer and a computer.

Telco

For those to whom size matters, telco was the place to be for deal activity. The usual suspects were out and about. Michael Malone at iiNet picked up Adam Internet for $60 million after the ACCC figured Telstra was probably a big enough telco as it was. The Canadians liked the look of our telecommunications margins and the Ontario Teachers Fund picked up 70% of Nextgen (getting Metronode and Infoplex as added extras) for $600 million.

Serial acquirers M2 came out early in the year with $200 million for Dodo and followed it up with grabbing Eftel for $44 million. Wireless broadband innovator, BigAir, acquired Intelligent IP with $10 million down and $10 million to pay, based on performance.

To cap off the year, it seems TPG Chief Executive, David Teoh, couldn't bear to see AAPT go through another Christmas Day without a suitor, easing New Zealand Telecom's pain to the tune of $450 million.

Online Retail

We know there will be winners in the online retail space, but it will come at a cost. Some showing real promise were Catch of the Day and OzSale, as well as The Iconic (fueled by a seemingly never ending geyser of marketing spend thanks to a $25 million injection early in the year by Summit Partners). This year Grays Online picked up $50 million in revenue with the acquisition of oo.com and seemed intent on establishing itself as Australia's largest pure play internet retailer. ASX-listed vehicle, Mnemon, is in the process of buying DealsDirect for $15 million.

Others have not fared so well. A number of media companies have moved away from their group-buying assets, while specialty online shoer, StyleTread, was sold to an Australian shoe dynasty, the Munro family.

With group-buying on the wane, the current heat is on taxi booking services, with both goCatch and Ingogo getting funding in the $3 million range and US giant Uber starting up in earnest in Australia.

The World Discovers Australia

If you want to get rich in Australian tech right now, create a product that fits into a US company's product suite and they will beat a path to your door. In my experience, the time has never been better to sell a business to the US or seek investment from US venture capitalists.

Fleetmatics bought Connect2Field. Intel bought Matt Barrie's former home, Sensory Networks, for $25 million, and resources software specialist, ISS Group, was snapped up by US tech services business P2ES for $38 million.

On the fund side, Revolution Growth pumped $40 million into Bigcommerce, and Boston headquartered private equity house TA Associates gave Macquarie and their co-investors a big win when they bought out Aussie software company Nintex for $213 million.

Consultants Bolt 'em On

The disruption caused by the internet has finally caught up with the consulting world and the big firms are looking for answers in acquisitions. Deloitte filled its boots with three Australian acquisitions this year: NXG Business Solutions, Quattro Innovation and web specialists Digicon.

PWC took out Booz & Co on a global basis and, in a novel move, Woolworths acquired 50% of big data consultancy, Quantium, for $20 million.

Telstra Gets Healthy

This year, Telstra invested a rumoured $25 million for 50% of health technology provider Fred IT; spent around $40 million to buy Database Consultants Australia's health division, and invested in electronic health operator, IP Health. Telstra recently partnered with Seven West Media to put $10 million into online health directory, HealthEngine.

Health aside, Telstra also spent $100 million on unified communications player, NSC Group, and invested $18 million in mobile applications developer Kony Solutions. The telco finished the year on a high note joining with a range of global players investing $100 million for 5% of DropBox competitor, Box.

The Public Market Reopens for Tech

iSelect got out of the gates early in the year, but hit some difficulties losing a CEO and attracting an ASIC probe. Accel-backed OzForex had a great listing and continues to look strong off the back of a stable business with a great growth profile. Freelancer went to 5x on its listing day briefly flirting with a $1 billion valuation before coming back a little. Earlier this month, IT services rollup PS&C raised $25 million, but closed down 10% on opening day, despite being heavily oversubscribed.

What's On the M&A Table for 2014

Given the halo effect of successful US-funded Australian tech companies like Atlassian, Bigcommerce and Nintex, we can expect more US fund interest in Australia in 2014.

Given the high stakes at play in the post-NBN world, there will be more consolidation in the sector.

In consulting, Deloitte seem hungrier than ever to expand by acquisition. As the internet continues its attack on the consulting world, expect to see more bolt-ons.

In Big Data, the Woolworths-Quantium deal has been looked at as a potential model for large consumer-facing corporates who are struggling to implement needle-moving big data projects internally. Lots of slide rulers being run over big data companies at the moment.

As for public listings, a float is definitely an option for some tech companies. SurfStitch is rumoured to be looking at a listing, and 2014 may even see Atlassian list in the US. Also mining is down, that means there will be lots of listed shells on the market available for backdoor listing. Expect to see our entrepreneurial brothers from the west re-birth their penny miners into high-growth cloud businesses – just like they did in dotcom days of old.

With all this activity and the positive outlook for the tech sector next year, I am reminded of the famous Silicon Valley bumper sticker "Please God – Just One More Bubble."

Article 7: Analysis of relative merits of listing on ASX or in the US

First published in *Sydney Morning Herald* on October 16, 2013 as

New York or ASX: The Team Entrepreneur's New Dilemma

http://www.theage.com.au/it-pro/it-opinion/new-york-or-asx-the-tech-entrepreneurs-new-dilemma-20131016-hv23e.html

Investors have long memories and many seem unable to forgive the Australian tech sector for the speedy evaporation of cash that occurred during the dotcom meltdown. However, 13 years on, there may be a glimmer of hope for the Australian tech IPO market. Last week, Ozforex finished its first day up 28% and, on Tuesday, Freelancer.com Chief Executive, Matt Barrie, listed the outsourcing marketplace on the Australian Stock Exchange after shunning a $430 million trade sale. He said a local listing was necessary to help foster the IT industry in Australia.

There is no doubt the Australian tech sector is experiencing something of a golden age, with fast growth success stories like Atlassian, BigCommerce and 99designs at the top end and an unprecedented level of activity in the start-up and incubator space.

You know things must be good when the debate occupying a number of entrepreneurs' minds is whether to list on the ASX or in the US – this has not been a big concern for the past decade as entrepreneurs' and investors' only real exit was a trade sale.

Matt Barrie says the ASX is the right place for Freelancer, while Atlassian's Mike Cannon-Brookes sees the US tech-heavy exchange, NASDAQ, as the natural home for his company. What are the arguments?

1. US Venture Capitalists Speak Louder

Many of the larger Australian tech companies have US venture capitalists on the share register and on tap for advice, and the reality is that US venture capitalists will make the decision they believe will lead to the greatest return. However, both Ozforex and New Zealand cloud accounting software flyer Xero listed on the ASX (Xero is also listed in New Zealand). Ozforex had US VC Accel Partners as an investor and Xero had Peter Thiel (PayPal founder and first external investor in Facebook).

2. Size Matters

The ASX is not seen to be big enough to allow a technology company to grow to its optimum size when compared to the NASDAQ.

Carsales, REA and Seek are obvious examples of Australian tech businesses that have grown into massive companies on the ASX. So, it is possible to grow big on the ASX; however, there are many more big and likeminded tech-related companies on the NASDAQ.

3. Analysts Count

ASX investors and analysts do not know how to value technology businesses. Excluding Telstra, the ASX has 127 technology and telecommunications companies with an aggregate market cap of approximately $30 billion. The NASDAQ has over 2,700 companies, the lion's share of which are tech-related. So, there is a much deeper market in the US and, consequently, better analyst coverage and understanding. Mike Cannon-Brookes has said of the ASX that it does not have a lot of software companies like his, and this is accurate.

4. Regulatory Burden

The ASX says that its onboarding and disclosure requirements are less onerous on companies than overseas exchanges. However, after the United States passed the JOBS (Jumpstart Our Business Start-ups) Act, many companies going public can get up to a five-year exemption from certain disclosure requirements.

It should be noted that the ASX has made a special effort to reach out to technology companies recently and we should certainly see more activity there.

5. Forget NASDAQ, what about NYSE?

As news comes overnight that Twitter has picked the New York Stock Exchange over NASDAQ for its listing, technology companies may have all three on their consideration list. The NYSE has experienced a resurgence in tech IPOs since that major technical glitch by NASDAQ marred the Facebook IPO. Recently, the NYSE also won the listings for LinkedIn, Yelp and Pandora.

So which exchange is right? The answer is "it depends" (said like a true lawyer). There will be a whole range of issues not limited to these.

The really great thing for anyone involved in technology in Australia however is that – at long last – we are again having a conversation about IPOs.

Article 8: Analysis of 2012 tech & telco deals

First published in the *Sydney Morning Herald/The Age* on 20 December 2012 as

2012 – The Year in Tech Deals

http://www.theage.com.au/it-pro/business-it/2012-the-year-in-tech-deals-20121220-2bowl.html

Mergers and acquisitions in technology and telecommunications businesses outpaced activity in other sectors this year. Bucking a general downturn in investment activity elsewhere, there was reasonable deal flow in online, media, telco and IT services. The US venture capital community even paid us a visit or two.

If the global economy turns, 2013 could be a very strong year for the sector. Below is a summary of the deals and some thoughts about where the opportunities are for 2013.

Online

The group-buying phenomenon came down to earth this year, after the Spreets-induced excitement of last year. Rumours persist of attempts at consolidation as some operators appear to be suffering, but few transactions have been consummated this year. Catchofthe-Day proved to be the most active, acquiring wine vertical Vinimofo and then making a big move into the online food ordering and delivery business with the acquisitions of EatNow, Takeaways.com.au and Mytable.com.au. The media machine went into dot-com era conniptions when the CEO suggested that the business was worth $600 million and might consider an IPO.

It seemed that online fashion was the place to be this year, with APN acquiring 82% of brandsExclusive, StyleTread picking up a $12 million Series C round, OzSale grabbing Buyinvite and Shoes of Prey coaxing $3 million from high profile US and Australian backers. The German accelerator, Rocket Internet made a big impact on the Australian market with The Iconic. Seemingly spending on marketing like it was 1999, The Iconic got a big boost when JP Morgan Asset Management invested almost $20 million for a piece of the fun.

Someone has to deliver all that couture and investors proved interested, with ShippingEasy receiving $2 million in venture funding and freight-play, Temando, receiving $5 million from Ellerston Capital.

Media Companies

Normally driving the digital M&A activity, the media companies were relatively reserved this year. Seven Group got out of the telco business once and for all with the sale of Vividwireless/Unwired to Singtel Optus for $230 million and the sale of VoIP pioneer, Engin to Eftel for $9 million.

Ten got into the second-screen business with social TV power-house, Zeebox, while Nine got to continue transmitting with no receiver. APN moved to 100% of NZ group-buying site, GrabOne and 50% of sports group buyer, My Team Deals. Fairfax [publisher of this site] was quiet on the acquisitions front, but sold the remarkable Trade Me asset, booking a big profit along the way. Full credit to former Fairfax CEO David Kirk for an inspired (if somewhat unpopular) decision to want to be the dominant online player in New Zealand all those years ago (well, 2006).

Journalists had little to be excited about this year as many of the media companies pared back newsrooms; however, hearts did flutter (and online news-related business plans were hastily cobbled together) when *News* bought finance journalist Alan Kohler's *Eureka Report* and *Business Spectator* for a reported $22 million.

Telecommunications

There can be few sectors more dynamic than telco in Australia at present. The national broadband network (NBN) rollout, mobile broadband growth and internet content delivery are just some of the factors driving opportunities in the market.

M2 went strongly, acquiring Primus for $192 million and Time Telecom for $18 million. Michael Malone from iiNet decided to top off last year's $60 million TransACT purchase with $105 million for broadband company Internode.

Boston-based PE firm, Riverside Partners, made a significant investment in Perth-based satellite communications business ITC Global which, in turn, acquired global satellite business, Spidersat Communications.

The recently created Applications & Ventures Group at Telstra wasted no time getting out of the blocks, with $5 million investments in online restaurant site, Dimmi (with Village Roadshow) and cloud-based contact centre business, IPscape. Their first foray into the US venture capital scene caused a big splash with the group leading a Series E round in video services provider Ooyala with a $35 million investment. Back home, Telstra surprised the market with the acquisition of low-cost South Australian ISP, Adam Internet, rumoured to have a price tag around $50 million. The deal is still subject to ACCC approval.

Optus acquired online restaurant site Eatability and, via its venture fund Innov8, has been making small investments into promising Australian start-ups, while mobile marketing innovator 5th Finger was sold to America's largest independent advertising agency, Merkle.

Technology

The past few years have seen strong moves by overseas IT services companies buying up Australian companies. This year, the trend continued with China's biggest outsourcer, HiSoft, buying the Australian arm of consulting firm, BearingPoint. Indian outsourcing giant, Wipro, improved its big data product offering by paying $35 million for analytics company, Promax Applications.

Japan's FujiFilm Holdings paid $375 million for Salmat's Business Process Outsourcing Division, while NEC acquired the technology solutions business of Australian IT firm, CSG, for $227 million.

US Venture Capital

The US Venture Capital funds have been scouring the Australian market looking for reasonable priced investments as Silicon Valley tech start-ups have quite full valuations these days. 2011 was a big year for US VC in Australia, with the likes of Accel Partners writing large cheques for stakes in 99designs, OzForex and Atlassian. However, despite the interest levels being high, 2012 did not herald any big investments other than General Catalyst investing a follow-on Series B $20 million in Bigcommerce.

There were small cheques being written, with mobile play Binu receiving $2 million from a syndicate led by Google Chairman, Eric Schmidt's Tomorrow Ventures, iPad property app start-up Happy Inspector getting $1 million from a group including 500 Startups, and Microsoft's Bing Fund making one of its first investments into an Australia gaming start-up, Pinion.

What to Watch Out For in 2013

Given the state of the advertising market, the media companies are unlikely to be big buyers; however, it will be interesting to see how digital pioneer Rohan Lund steers the Seven West Media Group as its recently appointed COO.

Leighton's are in the process of selling Nextgen. We wait to see which organisation can come up with the money to buy these assets and how they will get leveraged.

On the telco side, there is plenty to watch. Where will Deena Shiff take Telstra AVG? Austin Bryan at Singtel Optus has a global mandate and they have made some great investments offshore with Pixable and Amobee. Also TPG, iiNet and M2 rarely sit on the sidelines for long.

US VCs continue to visit our shores regularly and I think we can expect to see more investments being made by them, likely at the lower rather than the higher levels. Their interest is in highly scalable technology businesses with global potential. On that front, we might expect to see more announcements around Bigcommerce and Atlassian as they continue to grow strongly globally.

The group-buying market looks ready for consolidation and I would expect to see more movement there. In online apparel, one of the big questions is whether The Iconic continues its remarkable advertising spend.

The ex-dot-com-er in me wants to see CatchoftheDay's Leibovitch brothers get their $600 million IPO away, but I am not sure the market is quite ready for that.

Hills Holdings will be interesting to watch with Ted Pretty returning to the executive ranks as CEO. They acquired local IP security distributor LAN 1 this year and Ted has recently embarked on a significant restructure of this highly diversified company.

On the technology side, cloud technology will continue to be a driver, as companies seek acquisition opportunities which will give them cloud competence in vertical markets. Also, managed services will continue to be a focus, with offshore companies seeking to access Australia's still healthy (at least in comparison to the rest of the world) IT budgets and high dollar.

In summary, given the underlying changes in the market and the macro-trends, I think we can look forward to M&A in the tech and telco sector being up there with the most dynamic of the other sectors in 2013.

CHAPTER 5

Key Contacts in the Australian Tech Sector

1. Corporate Advisors

Company	Contact Name	Cities
Large		
Citigroup	Various	Sydney, Melbourne, Brisbane
Credit Suisse Emerging Markets	Gavan Carroll	Sydney, Melbourne, Perth
Deloitte	Damien Tampling/Mike Tilson	Sydney, Barton, Brisbane, Melbourne, Perth, Adelaide, Hobart, Darwin
EY	Charlie Lewis/Colin McNeil	Sydney, Brisbane, Melbourne, Canberra, Perth, Adelaide
Fort Street Advisers	Ben Keeble	Sydney

Company	Contact Name	Cities
Goldman Sachs	Various	Sydney, Melbourne
Grant Samuel	Damien Elias	Sydney, Melbourne
JP Morgan	Various	Sydney, Melbourne
KPMG	Peter Turner/Toby Gardner	Sydney, Brisbane, Adelaide, Gold Coast, Canberra, Melbourne, Perth, Darwin, Hobart
Macquarie Group	Various	Sydney, Melbourne, Brisbane
UBS Emerging Markets	Peter Nelson/Luke Bentvelzen/Udai Chopra/Adrian Lee	Brisbane, Melbourne, Perth, Sydney
Boutique		
Asia Principal Capital	Philip King	Singapore
Callafin	Vivian Stewart/ Tony Sullivan/Dominic Ryan	Sydney
CLSA/Citic	Mark Dorney	Melbourne, Sydney
CMB Captial	Jamie Olsen/ Tristram Clemison	Sydney, Melbourne
Delling Advisory	Nick Ellsmore	Sydney
Federation Capital	Iain Maine/Scott Anderson	Sydney
Hall Capital	David Hall/David Rampa/ David Burkett/Matt Rogers	Sydney
Illuminate Capital	Paul Lowry	Sydney, Perth

Company	Contact Name	Cities
Inanda Partners	Grant Smuts	Sydney
Inteq	Kim Jacobs	Sydney
Jacanda	Andrew Sandes/ Jay Hennock	Sydney
KTM Capital	Keith Kerridge/Todd McGrouther/Charles Lindop	Sydney
Mannagum Capital	David Willington	Sydney
Nectar Partners	James Mollison	Sydney
Newport Capital	Lou Richard/ Bradley Keeling	Sydney
Nextec	Richard Gibson/Neil Bourne	Sydney
Overture Capital	Philip Alexander	Sydney
Pier Capital	Richard Kuo	Sydney
Pottinger	Nigel Lake/Cassandra Kelly/Andrew Paddon	Sydney
Record Point	Michael Firmin	Sydney, San Francisco
Scancorp	Ian Knight	Brisbane, Melbourne
ShineWing Australia (Formerly Moore Stephens)	Tony Schiavello	Sydney, Brisbane, Melbourne, Canberra, Perth, Adelaide
Sydney Capital Partners	Stuart Anderson	Sydney
TMT Partners	Mark Burns/Hugh Richards	Sydney
Venture Advisory	Rob Antulov/Philip Alexander	Sydney, Melbourne

2. Australian Tech-Focussed Venture Capital Funds

Company Name	Website Address
Adventure Capital	www.adventurecapital.vc
Airtree	www.airtreevc.com
AMP Ventures	www.amp.com.au
Artesian Venture Partners	www.artesianinvest.com
Bailador	www.bailador.com.au
Blackbird	www.blackbird.vc
Blacksheep Capital	www.blacksheepcapital.com.au
Blue Sky Ventures	www.blueskyfunds.com.au
Carthona Capital	www.carthonacapital.com
Citrix Ventures	www.citrix.com
Founder Institute	www.fi.co
GBS Ventures	www.gbsventures.com.au
Green Lane Digital	www.greenlanedigital.com.au
Intel Capital	www.intelcapital.com
Jolimont Capital	www.jolimontcapital.com.au
Jungle Capital	www.junglecapital.com.au
M.H. Carnegie & Co	www.mhcarnegie.com
Macquarie Bank	www.macquarie.com.au/mgl/au
One Ventures	www.one-ventures.com.au
Optus Innov8	www.optusinnov8seed.com.au
Rampersand	www.rampersand.com
Reinventure	www.reinventure.com.au
Right Click Capital	www.rightclickcapital.com
Riverside Ventures	www.riversidepartners.com
Scale Investors	www.scaleinvestors.com.au
Sketchbook Ventures	www.sketchbookventures.com.au

Company Name	Website Address
Southern Cross Venture Partners	www.sxvp.com
Square Peg Capital	www.squarepegcap.com
Starfish	www.starfishvc.com
Sydney Seed Fund	www.sydneyseedfund.com.au
Telstra Ventures	www.telstra.com.au/ventures
Venture Crowd	www.venturecrowd.com.au
Wholesale Investor	www.wholesaleinvestor.com.au
Yarra Capital Partners	www.ycp.com.au

3. Asian Tech-Focussed Venture Capital Funds

Company Name	Website Address
1337 Ventures	www.1337accelerator.com
Acumen Ventures Adelaide	www.acumenvc.com
Ardent Ventures	www.ardentcap.com
BlueHill Asset Management	www.bluehill.com.sg
Celfino Ltd	www.celfino.de
Convergence Ventures	www.convergencevc.com
East Ventures	www.east.vc
Far East Ventures	www.fareast.ventures
Fenox Venture Capital	www.fenoxvc.com
Frontier Accelerator	www.frontieraccelerator.com
Golden Gate Ventures	www.goldengate.vc
GREE Ventures	www.greeventures.com/en
Impact Ventures	www.impactventures.net
Kickstart Ventures	www.kickstart.ph
KK Fund	kkfund.co
Life.SREDA VC	www.lifesreda.com

Company Name	Website Address
Malaysia Venture Capital Management	www.mavcap.com
Mirin Capital	www.mirin.vc
Monk's Hill Ventures	www.monkshill.com
Morph Ventures	www.morphventures.com
NSI Ventures	www.nsi.vc
Proficeo Ventures	www.proficeo.com
Simile Venture Partners	www.simileventure.com
Spaze Ventures Pte Ltd	www.startupspaze.com
TNF Ventures	www.tnfventures.com
Vickers Venture Partners	www.vickersventure.com

4. Australian Seed/Angel Investment Organisations

Company Name	Website Address
Adelaide Angel Investors	www.angel.co/#adelaide/investors
Aurelius Digital	www.aureliusdigital.com.au
Australian Association of Angel Investors	www.aaai.net.au
Australian Investment Network	www.australianinvestmentnetwork.com
Brisbane Angels	www.brisbaneangels.com.au
Innovation Bay	www.innovationbay.com
Investors' Organisation	www.investorsorg.com
Melbourne Angels	www.melbourneangels.net
Optus-Innov8 Seed Program	www.optusinnov8seed.com.au
Sydney Angels	www.sydneyangels.net.au
The Creative Enterprise Fund	www.creativeenterprise.com.au/investment
WA Angel Investors	www.waai.net.au

5. Australian Pitch Competitions

Company Name	Website Address
Innovation Bay	www.innovationbay.com
RiverPitch Brisbane	riverpitch.com
Slush	www.slush.org
SydStart	sydstart.wordpress.com
Tech23	www.tech23.com.au

6. US Venture Capitalists with an interest in Australian Tech Companies

Company Name	Website Address
Accel Partners	www.accel.com
Accel - KKR	www.accel-kkr.com
August Capital	www.augustcap.com
Battery Ventures	www.battery.com
Founders Fund	www.foundersfund.com
General Catalyst Partners	www.generalcatalyst.com
Insight Venture Partners	www.insightpartners.com
Lightspeed Ventures	www.lsvp.com
Partners for Growth	www.pfgrowth.com
Quest Venture Partners	www.questvp.com
Revolution Growth	www.revolution.com
Sequoia Capital	www.sequoiacap.com
Shasta Ventures	www.shastaventures.com
Sierra Ventures	www.sieraventures.com
Spectrum Equity	www.spectrumequity.com
Technology Crossover Ventures	www.tcv.com
Valar Ventures	www.valar.com

Company Name	Website Address
Vector Capital	www.vectorcapital.com
Western Technology Investments	www.westerntech.com

Australian Incubators

Company Name	Website Address	Cities where they operate/based in Aust
Angel Cube	www.angelcube.com	Melbourne
ANZ Innovyz-START	www.innovyzstart.com	Adelaide
Atomic Sky	www.atomicsky.com.au	Perth
ATP Innovations	www.atp-innovations.com.au	Sydney
Blue Chilli	www.bluechilli.com	Sydney, Melbourne
Brisbane Technology Park	www.btpinfo.com.au	Brisbane
Creative Industries Innovation Centre	www.creativeinnovation.net.au	Sydney
Digital 4ge	www.digital4ge.com	Sydney
Gold Coast Innovation Centre	www.wptraining.net.au/gcic	Gold Coast
Ignition Labs	www.ignitionlabs.com.au	Sydney
iLab	www.ilabaccelerator.com	Brisbane
Innovation Centre	www.innovationcentre.com.au	Sunshine Coast
Muru - D	www.muru-d.com	Sydney
New Ventures Institute at Flinders University	www.nviflinders.com.au	Perth

Company Name	Website Address	Cities where they operate/based in Aust
Pollenizer	www.pollenizer.com	Sydney
PushStart	www.pushstart.com.au	Multiple cities
QUT Creative Enterprise Australia	www.creativeenterprise.com.au	Brisbane
Small Technologies Cluster	www.stcaustralia.org	Melbourne
Spacecubed Intensify Scholarship	www.spacecubed.com	Perth
Startmate	www.startmate.com.au	Sydney
Startup Tasmania	www.startuptasmania.com	Hobart
Venture Incubator Space	www.cse.unsw.edu.au/engage-with-us/graduates-alumni	Sydney
York Butter Factory	www.yorkbutterfactory.com	Melbourne

Australian Accelerators

Company Name	Website Address	Cities where they operate/based in Aust
25Fifteen	www.25fifteen.com	Sydney
Amcom Upstart	www.amcomupstart.com.au	Perth
AWI Ventures	www.awiventures.com	Sydney
Griffin Accelerator	www.griffinaccelerator.com.au	Canberra

Company Name	Website Address	Cities where they operate/based in Aust
Slingshot Jumpstart	www.slingshotters.com	Sydney
Springboard Enterprises Australia	www.sb.co/programs/australia	Sydney

Australian Co-working Spaces

Company Name	Website Address	Cities where they operate/based in Aust
ATP Innovations	www.atp-innovations.com.au	Sydney
Collins Collective	www.collinscollective.com.au	Melbourne
Depo8	www.depo8.com	Melbourne
Fishburners	www.fishburners.org	Sydney
Henly Club	www.henley-club.com.au	Melbourne
iCentral	www.sydstart.wordpress.com/icentral	Sydney
Inspire9	www.inspire9.com	Melbourne
Majoran Distillery	www.majoran.co	Adelaide
Manly Emporium	_	Sydney
Queens Collective	www.queenscollective.com	Melbourne
Revolver Creative	www.revolvercreative.com.au	Melbourne
Start Nest	www.startnest.com	Sydney

Company Name	Website Address	Cities where they operate/based in Aust
Stone and Chalk	www.stone-andchalk.com.au	Sydney
Tank Stream Labs	tankstreamlabs.com	Sydney
Teamsquare	teamsquarehq.com	Melbourne
The Cluster	www.theclus-ter.com.au/#	Melbourne
Vibewire	www.vibewire.org	Sydney
York Butter Factory	www.yorkbutterfac-tory.com	Melbourne
Springboard Enterprises Australia	www.sb.co/programs/australia	Sydney

Ancillary Services

Accountants

Company	Contact Name	Cities
Azzure Group	Michael Derin	Sydney, Gold Coast
CharterNet	Sameer Kas-sam/Saeed Mir-zakhani	Sydney

Company	Contact Name	Cities
Crowe Horwarth	Angus Stewart	Sydney, Melbourne, Perth, Adelaide, Brisbane, Gold Coast, Hobart
Deloitte Private	Josh Tanchel/Troy Wilson	Adelaide, Canberra, Darwin, Sydney, Melbourne, Hobart, Perth, Brisbane
Grant Thorton	Simon Coulton/Les Corder	Adelaide, Perth, Brisbane, Cairns, Sydney, Melbourne
Hall Chadwick	David Kenney	Sydney, Melbourne, Gold Coast, Brisbane, Perth, Darwin
Moore Stephens	Anthony Andersen	Sydney, Brisbane, Melbourne, Canberra, Perth, Adelaide
Verde Group	Rachel White	Sydney, Gold Coast

Lawyers

For a list of tech focused lawyers, please go to www.lawpath.com

Employment Agencies

Company	Contact Name	Cities
Finite	Tracy Thompson, Duncan Thomson	All Aust cities
HarveyNash	Francisco Morales	Sydney
Mitchell Lake	Phaedon Stough, Kevin Griffiths	Sydney, Melbourne, San Francisco
Recruit Loop		Sydney

PR Agencies

Company	Contact Name	Cities
Click PR	Vuki Vujasinovic, Rob Langford	Sydney
Media & Capital Partners	Asher Moses	Sydney
PR Group	Caroline/Melissa Shawyer	Melbourne, Sydney

CHAPTER 6

List of Australian Tech, Media & Telco Deals 2012-2015

Summary of Mergers & Acquisitions in the Australian TMT Sectors

1. Internet deals 86

2. Telecommunications deals 103

3. Media & content deals... 111

4. Software & information technology deals............. 123

5. US venture capital deals... 146

6. Initial public offerings.. 149

7. Back door listings 153

1. Internet deals

Year	Target	Buyer	Value	Details
2015	SeekAsia Limited and OCC Mundial D.R.	SEEK Limited	AU$161M	SEEK Limited the Australian based provider of online employment classifieds has acquired a 5.2% stake in SeekAsia Limited and a 41.8% stake in OCC Mundial D.R. a Mexico based company providing online recruitment services.
2015	Hall	Atlassian	N/A	Atlassian, the Australian based software development platform provider has acquired Hall a US based online chat service provider.
2015	Airtasker	Morning Crest Captial and others	AU$6.5M	Australian based marketplace Airtasker has raised AU$6.5M in funding from Morning Crest Capital and others.
2015	Sendle.com	National Roads and Motorists Association (NRMA) and others	AU$1.8M	Sendle.com a door-to-door parcel delivery company has raised AU$1.8M in funding from NRMA and others.
2015	Edrolo	AirTree Ventures	AU$2.6M	Online education provider Edrolo has received an AU$2.6M investment from AirTree Ventures.
2015	Moula Money	Liberty Financial and others	AU$30M	Moula Money an online small business lender has raised AU$30M in funding from Liberty Financial and others.
2015	Tripalocal	Euler Capital LLC	AU$850K	Tripalocal, an Australian company that offers online trip booking services has raised $850K in order to fund its expansion in China.

86

1. Internet

Year	Target	Buyer	Value	Details
2015	Ingogo	VentureCrowd and others	AU$12M	Ingogo the Australian based taxi booking and payment platform has raised $12 million in funding, including $4.2 million from crowd equity platform VentureCrowd.
2015	TidyMe	Airtree Ventures	AU$750K	TidyMe, an Australian startup has raised $750K from Airtree Ventures a $60 million tech fund.
2015	Redbubble Ltd	Private equity	AU$16M	Private equity buyers have acquired an undisclosed stake in Redbubble Ltd an Australian based online marketplace for independent artists.
2015	Dimmi	TripAdvisor	AU$25M	Dimmi, an Australina start up that provides an online restaurant booking service has been acquired by TripAdvisor the travel review website.
2015	Outware Mobile	Melbourne IT	AU$21.7M	Melbourne IT an Australian based company that provides domain name registration has acquired a 50.2% stake in app developer Outware Mobile.
2015	OCC Mundial and SeekAsia Limited	SEEK Limited	AU$161M	SEEK Limited an Australian online job listing and training platform has acquired a 41.8% stake in OCC Mundial a Mexico base company that operates an online recruitment service and a 5.2% stake in SeekAsia an Australian based acquisition vehicle created by SEEK Limited and others.
2015	Magicseaweed Ltd and Rolling Youth Press Pty Ltd	SurfStitch Group Limited	AU$21M	SurfStitch the Australian based company that markets and sells surf clothing online has acquired Magicseaweed a UK based website that provides surfing information and Rolling Youth Press an Australian based company that provides online surfing information.
2015	Menulog Pty Ltd	JUST EAT plc	AU$853	JUST EAT plc the UK based online restaurant delivery marketplace has acquired Menulog an Australian based company that provides an online takeaway platform.

1. Internet

Year	Target	Buyer	Value	Details
2015	Careerone Pty Limited	Acquire Learning Pty Ltd	AU$20M	Acquire Learning, an Australian company engaged in education has acquired an 80% stake in Careerone Pty Limited an Australian based online job listing platform.
2015	Arnold Travel Technology Pty Limited	Serko Limited	N/A	Arnold Travel Technology Pty Ltd, the Australian based online travel booking website has been acquired by Serko Limited a New Zealand based online travel booking site for an undisclosed sum.
2015	RateSetter	carsales.com	$10M	Carsales.com, the online classifieds company, has acquired a 20% stake in RateSetter a peer-to-peer lender.
2015	OpenLearning	Clive Mayhew and others	$1.7M	Clive Mayhew (who previously sold Sky Software) and others have invested in Australian start-up OpenLearning a Massive Open Online Course (MOOC) provider.
2015	UberGlobal	MelbourneIT	$15.5M	Australian based domain name registration company MelbourneIT has acquired UberGlobal, Australia's third largest cloud service provider.
2015	Temando Pty Ltd	Neopost SA	$50M	Neopost, a French-based company producing mailroom equipment, has acquired an undisclosed stake in Temando an Australian based company that provides an e-commerce platform for freight quoting.
2015	Word of Mouth Online	Oneflare	N/A	Oneflare, an online job marketplace, has acquired Word of Mouth Online. Word of Mouth Online is the largest online review site in Australia.
2015	Adage	Oneshift	N/A	Australian start-up Oneshift, an online job network, has acquired Australian-based Adage, which also provides an online job network but is targeted at a mature market.

1. Internet

Year	Target	Buyer	Value	Details
2015	Anywhere Healthcare	Telstra Health	N/A	Telstra Health has acquired Anywhere Healthcare. Anywhere Healthcare provides people in remote areas of Australia with access to specialist health care professionals.
2014	Occasional Butler	Airtasker	N/A	Online tasks marketplace Airtasker has acquired Australian-based jobs outsourcing website Occasional Butler.
2014	Pawshake	AirTree Ventures	$1.5M	AirTree Ventures, an Australian-based venture capital fund, has invested $1.5M in Pawshake. Pawshake connects pet owners with potential pet-sitters.
2014	brandsExclusive (Australia) Pty Ltd	AussieCommerce	N/A	Aussie Commerce, an Australian-based company, engaged in e-commerce has acquired brandsExclusive (Australia) Pty Ltd the Australian-based company engaged in e-commerce.
2014	Dailydo	AussieCommerce	N/A	AussieCommerce, the Australian e-commerce business has acquired Dailydo the New Zealand diversified e-commerce group.
2014	Stratton	Carsales.com	$60.1M	Carsales.com, the Australian online car classifieds has acquired online lender and prominent Carsales advertiser Stratton.
2014	SurfStitch Pty Ltd and Swell Inc	Consortium of investors including the founders of SurfStitch	$32M	A consortium of investors has acquired Swell Inc, an online retailer of surf gear in the US along with a 51% stake in SurfStitch Pty Ltd an online Australian based retailer of surfing accessories.
2014	Betfair Australasia Pty Ltd	Crown Resorts Limited	$9M	Crown Resorts Limited, the Australian gaming company has acquired a 50% stake in Betfair Australasia Pty Limited, the Australian online gaming exchange platform.
2014	Strategic Payments Services	Cuscal	$37.4M	Cuscal will buy Strategic Payments service and merge with it to create one joint entity that will target the mobile payments market.

1. Internet

Year	Target	Buyer	Value (AU)	Details
2014	Professional Performance System Pty Ltd	Disruptive Investment Group Ltd	N/A	Disruptive Investment Group has acquired a 54.69% stake in Professional Performance System, owner of BYOjet Group, one of Australia's largest online travel agents.
2014	Hipages.com.au	Ellerston Capital	$6M	James Packer's former personal investment vehicle, Ellerston Capital, along with KTM Capital and Australian Ethical Investment have acquired a AU$6M minority stake in home improvements classifieds website hipages.com.au.
2014	Wotif.com Holdings Limited	Expedia Inc	$703M	Expedia, the US online travel website, has acquired the Australian online travel website Wotif.com after approval was given by the ACCC.
2014	fantero.com	Freelancer Limited	N/A	Freelancer Limited has acquired the virtual content marketplace, fantero.com, including certain intellectual property and domain name assets. The Fantero network has over 100,000 members and consists of almost 1 million items of digital content including stock photos, web templates, audio, flash & video files, 3D models, plugins and scripts, and graphics and vector files.
2014	Blinkbox Music	Guvera	$7.6M	Tesco, the UK listed retailer, has sold its music streaming subsidiary Blinkbox Music to Australian based Guvera.
2014	Search Results Group	Invigor Group Limited	$5.8M	Invigor Group has acquired the Search Results Group, an Australian online media agency offering web development and marketing products.

1. Internet

Year	Target	Buyer	Value (AU)	Details
2014	Web24 Group Pty Ltd	j2 Global Inc	N/A	j2 Global, the global provider of internet services, has acquired the assets of Web24 Group an Australian company providing domain name and web hosting services.
2014	SR7	KPMG Australia	N/A	KPMG Australia has acquired Australian-based social media intelligence company SR7 for an undisclosed amount.
2014	Eskander's Betstar Pty Limited	Ladbrokes Plc	$22M	Ladbrokes Plc, a listed UK-based betting and gaming company, has acquired Eskander's Betstar Pty Limited, an Australian based company that provides internet and phone betting.
2014	Stay at Home Mum website	Leon Serry	N/A	Leon Serry, Melbourne-based investor, has reportedly captured a 30% stake in this domestic cooking blog which is currently seeking further equity investors having reportedly raised AU$3M to date.
2014	NetRegistry Pty Ltd	Melbourne IT Limited	$50M	Melbourne IT Limited, Australian based company that provides domain name registrations and online solutions has acquired NetRegistry Pty Ltd an Australian based internet services company.
2014	LoveByte	Migme	N/A	Migme, the ASX listed social entertainment platform has acquired LoveByte, a Singapore-based mobile applications business.
2014	Tagroom.com	MOKO Social Media Limited	N/A	MOKO Social Media, a provider of mobile social community platforms, has acquired an 80% stake in Australian-based news and entertainment website Tagroom.com
2014	Invitetobuy.dk	MySale Group	N/A	MySale Group, a leading online retailer, providing flash sales in Australia has acquired 60% of Scandinavia's leading flash sale website invitetobuy.dk

1. Internet

Year	Target	Buyer	Value (AU)	Details
2014	Posse, Beat the Q and e-Coffee Card	N/A	N/A	Posse, a social media site, Beat the Q a mobile ordering application and e-Coffee Card a loyalty card application are set to combine to offer a one-stop -shopping app.
2014	Intrepica	Nine Entertainment	$6M	Nine Entertainment has acquired a 30% stake in the education business Intrepica.
2014	Bullseye	Ogilvy	N/A	Ogilvy has acquired integrated digital marketing and technology services company Bullseye.
2014	OneShift	Programmed	$5M	OneShift, an Australian based online recruitment site for short-term employment opportunities has received AU$5M in funding from Programmed, a staffing management company.
2014	iProperty	Realestate.com.au	$106M	Realestate.com.au has bought a 17.2% stake in South East Asia property business iProperty.
2014	Fitlink	Reeltime Media	N/A	Reeltime Media has acquired Fitlink, an independent college offering fitness training courses online.
2014	Oasis Active	rsvp.com.au Pty Ltd	$90M	Fairfax's RSVP online dating site has merged with Oasis Active, with the aim of expanding its presence offshore. The deal gives Fairfax a controlling stake of 58%, Ten Network Holdings 17%, with the founders of Oasis to have 14%.
2014	Blue Chilli	Simon Hackett and Myer Family Investments	$5M	Simon Hackett and Myer Family Investments have invested AU$5M into Blue Chilli an Australian start-up accelerator.
2014	Surfdome.com	SurfStitch	$45M	SurfStitch, an Australian online retailer, has acquired Surfdome.com, a European online sports retailer.
2014	AdNear	Telstra	N/A	Telstra has invested in AdNear, a leading location intelligence company.

1. Internet

Year	Target	Buyer	Value (AU)	Details
2014	Bigcommerce	Telstra	N/A	Telstra has invested in Bigcommerce, a specialist in e-commerce and will help Bigcommerce in its bid to increase its market share in Australia.
2014	Panviva	Telstra	N/A	Telstra has invested in Panviva, a developer of process guidance software solutions aimed at simplifying the interactions between call centre staff and back office staff.
2014	DocuSign	Telstra	N/A	Telstra has made an undisclosed investment into US start-up DocuSign, a company that provides for individuals to use digital signatures in documents.
2014	Elemental	Telstra	N/A	Telstra has made an equity investment in Elemental, a supplier of software-defined video solutions for multiscreen content delivery. Telstra expects this technology to become in-creasingly popular with end-users viewing content on multiple devices.
2014	Orion Health Group Limited	Telstra Health	$20M	Telstra Health has stepped up its presence in the eHealth market by making a NZ$20M in-vestment into Orion Health Group Limited, an eHealth provider that recently listed on the New Zealand stock exchange.
2014	Cloud9 Software	Telstra Health	N/A	Telstra Health has acquired Cloud9 Software, an Australian based cloud software developer.
2014	Medinexus	Telstra Health	N/A	Telstra Health has acquired Medinexus a radiology and pathology secure messaging service.
2014	iCareHealth	Telstra Health	N/A	Telstra Health has acquired aged health software developer iCareHealth
2014	All Homes Pty Ltd	The Domain Group	$50M	The Domain Group, an Australian based company that operates real estate portals and a do-main business of Fairfax Media Limited, has acquired All Homes Pty Ltd, an Australian-based company that owns and operates an online property portal.

1. Internet

Year	Target	Buyer	Value (AU)	Details
2014	Viator	TripAdvisor	US$200M	Sydney-founded and now US based online tour agency Viator has been acquired by online travel site TripAdvisor.
2014	Oneflare	Various investors including Equity Venture Partners, Sydney Seed Fund and The Strategy Group	AU$1.5M	Oneflare has raised AU$1.5M in two years in the form of venture capital. Oneflare is an online local services marketplace startup based in Sydney.
2014	Nabo	Various parties including Re-inventure Group and Seven West Media	AU$2.25M	Nabo, an online social media network that connects neighbours, has received AU$2.25M in start-up funding from various parties including Reinventure Group and Seven West Media.
2014	goCatch	Venture capital firm Square Peg and others	AU$4.5M	Increased financial support for a new start-up application developer looking to compete in the taxi booking and payment market.
2014	SunHotels Group	Webjet	N/A	Webjet has acquired SunHotels Group, an online hotel provider in European resort destinations
2014	SocietyOne	Westpac Banking Corporation	AU$5M	Westpac Banking Corporation's new venture capital fund Reinventure Group has invested $5M in Australia's first peer-to-peer lender SocietyOne.
2013	Facilitate Digital Holdings Limited	Adslot Limited	AU$15M	Adslot Limited, an Australian company, engaged in operating the display media, search media and web development segment has acquired Facilitate Digital Holdings, an Australian company engaged in developing software for digital marketing.

DIGITAL DISRUPTION IN AUSTRALIA • 95

1. Internet

Year	Target	Buyer	Value (AU)	Details
2013	iCar Asia	Carsales.com	AU$13.4M	Carsales.com Limited has taken a 19.9% stake in iCar Asia Limited. iCar Asia owns and operates a network of online automotive websites in Thailand, Malaysia and Indonesia.
2013	oo.com.au	Grays Australia	N/A	Grays has purchased oo.com.au, an online department store, with the aim of becoming the country's largest pure-play online retailer by turnover. The deal is expected to increase Grays' annual sales by $50 million.
2013	Stayz Pty Ltd	HomeAway Inc	AU$220M	Following a competitive sale process Fairfax Media Limited sold 100% of Stayz Pty Limited, a wholly-owned subsidiary, to HomeAway Australia Holdings Pty Ltd, that is in turn a wholly-owned subsidiary of HomeAway Inc.
2013	Adam Internet Pty. Ltd.	iiNet Ltd	AU$60M	iiNet Ltd, the listed Australia-based company, engaged in the provision of Internet and telephony services, has agreed to acquire Adam Internet Pty. Ltd., the Australia-based provider of internet services. The acquisition will enable iiNet to further expand its consumer base to over 900,000 broadband subscribers and strengthens its position in the Australian market. Adam Internet will add a new data centre and additional DSLAM and fibre network infrastructure to iiNet. Post-acquisition, iiNet will retain all the staff of Adam Internet.
2013	goCatch	James Packer, Paul Bassat, the Libermans and the Kahlbetzers	AUS$3M	Financial support for the new taxi technology to compete against the dominance of industry giant Cabcharge. The taxi hailing app goCatch provides booking and payment services on smartphones and undermines the 10 per cent surcharge fee charged by Cabcharge.

1. Internet

Year	Target	Buyer	Value (AU)	Details
2013	DealsDirect.com.au	Mnemon Limited	AU$15M	Mnemon Limited, an Australia-based company that provides mobile personalisation, entertainment and technology services has acquired DealsDirect.com.au, the Australia-based online discount store.
2013	StyleTread	Munro family (private company)	N/A	The private Melbourne-based Munro family has acquired StyleTread for an undisclosed amount. The Munro family owns well-known brands such as Django & Juliette, I Love Billy, and others and also operates a chain of shoe stores.
2013	Best Recipes	News Corp Australia	N/A	News Limited Australia has acquired Best Recipes, an Australia-based company that provides online information about recipes.
2013	Interact Learning Pty Ltd	Open Universities Australia	N/A	Open Universities Australia has acquired 100 per cent interest in Interact Learning Pty Ltd, trading as e3Learning, a leading online training and compliance provider to Australia's corporate sector. The acquisition reflects OUA's strategic objective to broaden its student offering, as well as meeting corporate demand for education, training and compliance.
2013	Ebook Library	ProQuest LLC	AU$30M	ProQuest has agreed to acquire Ebook Library, the Australia-based provider of online catalogue books to academic and research libraries.
2013	Tiger Pistol	Rampersand	AU$1M	Australian start-up Tiger Pistol, a social media marketing platform has raised $1 million from Australian venture capital fund Rampersand in order to establish an office in Silicon Valley.
2013	1Form Online Pty Ltd	REA Group	AU$15M	1Form Online allows prospective tenants to apply for multiple properties using a single online form, it also provides data to real estate agents and online property sites including REA Group's realestate.com.au.

1. Internet

Year	Target	Buyer	Value (AU)	Details
2013	Box	Telstra	AU$10M	Telstra was one of several investors that acquired a combined 5% stake in Box, which is a US-based online storage service competing against Dropbox and plans to expand its global operations.
2013	HealthEngine	Telstra and Seven West Media	AU$10.4M	Both Telstra and Seven West Media will invest AU$5.2M each to secure an undisclosed stake in HealthEngine. HealthEngine claims to be Australia's largest online health directory and Telstra and Seven West hope to capitalise on Australia's growing healthcare sector with this investment.
2013	We Are Hunted	Twitter	N/A	We Are Hunted allows users to discover, play and share music online. It is expected that Twitter will use this acquisition to allow its users to discover new artists, listen to and buy music.
2013	MYOB hosting business	UberGlobal	N/A	Hosting and cloud services provider UberGlobal has acquired MYOB's domain and hosting business. This deal comprises the hosting brands SmartyHost and Ilisys.
2013	Ingogo	UBS & private equity funds	AU$3.4M	UBS and unnamed private equity funds invested $3.4 million in Ingogo, a 2-year-old start-up valued by UBS at $25 million and a competitor to the Cabcharge network, allowing consumers to call and pay for taxis using an app.
2013	Tom Water-house NT Pty Ltd	William Hill Plc	AU$40M	William Hill Plc, a UK based firm offering gaming, betting, online casino and poker sites, has acquired Tom Waterhouse NT Pty Ltd. The acquisition is part of William Hill's strategy to expand its business in international market. Tom Waterhouse will remain as managing director.
2012	Friendorse	APN	N/A	APN has taken a 25% stake in Friendorse following a successful trial of the start-up.
2012	GrabOne	APN News & Media	N/A	GrabOne, a NZ-based group buying website, was initially an Australia-based joint venture between APN News & Media and Shane Bradley. APN has bought out Bradley's stake in GrabOne.

1. Internet

Year	Target	Buyer	Value (AU)	Details
2012	MyTeamDeals	APN News & Media	N/A	APN Media has moved on another digital asset, picking up 50% of group buying site MyTeamDeals, a group buying platform for sporting clubs.
2012	brandsExclusive	APN News & Media Limited	$36M	APN has taken an 82% stake in brandsExclusive, an online retailer of heavily discounted premium brands.
2012	StartHere	Aura Capital	N/A	An online business which offers cash back deals on consumer electronics and household products founded by internet entrepreneur Adir Shiffman has just taken a stake from private equity group Aura Capital.
2012	TradeMe	Australian and NZ institutions	$616M	Fairfax Media has sold its 51 per cent holding in New Zealand online auction site Trade Me for $3.05 a share to raise $616 million to leave the company debt free. The stake was sold to a range of institutions in a placement through UBS. UBS sold the shares to a range of Australian and New Zealand institutions.
2012	SiteMinder	Bailador Investment Management	$5M	Online hotel distribution company SiteMinder has secured an investment from Bailador Investment Management.
2012	Allegro Networks	BigAir Group	$7.5M	Fixed wireless carrier BigAir Group acquired Allegro Networks, a Queensland based Telecommunications carrier founded in 2005 that has its fixed wired network coverage over South East Queensland.
2012	EatNow	CatchOfTheDay	N/A	The Catch Group will pay an undisclosed sum to buy EatNow, which was founded by Melbourne entrepreneur Matt Dyer. As part of the transaction, Catch has also bought online food ordering platform Takeaways.com.au and takeaway ordering site Mytable.com.au, giving it specific technologies and functions to be incorporated into the EatNow site. Mr Dyer and the other website founders will retain minority interests in the EatNow business.

1. Internet

Year	Target	Buyer	Value (AU)	Details
2012	Vinomofo	CatchOfTheDay Group	N/A	CatchOfTheDay Group, the James Packer-based daily deals group, has acquired Vinomofo, which is an Adelaide based online wine retailer for an undisclosed sum.
2012	Temando	Ellerston Capital	$5M	Brisbane-based Freight aggregator Temando has secured an investment from James Packer's investment fund, Ellerston Capital.
2012	Qanda Webspy Business	Festvue Inc	$1M	The Webspy Business is involved in the transformation of raw data, stored in log files, into manageable information, that can provide clients with a view of their Internet, email, and network usage.
2012	Imorial.com and EventArc.com	Future Capital Development Fund	N/A	Domenic Carosa's Future Capital Development Fund has invested in two online start-ups – a memorial site for people and pets (Imorial.com) and an event registration and ticketing platform (EventArc.com). Imorial.com allows users to create free online memorial and EventArc.com is a self-service online event registration and ticketing platform.
2012	Shoes of Prey Pty Ltd	Global syndicate	US$3M	Shoes of Prey, an online mass customisation retailer of shoes, allowing consumers to design, buy and share their own bespoke shoes, announced it has secured funding from a global syndicate, including Silicon Valley's high-profile players such as TechCrunch founder Mike Arrington's investment company CrunchFund, Bill Tai and Atlassian founder Mike Cannon-Brookes.
2012	Quikflix Ltd	Home Box Office, Inc	AU$10M	Home Box Office has acquired a 16% stake in Quikflix Ltd, an Australia-based online movie rental company, in exchange for 83.3 million preference shares.
2012	The Iconic	JP Morgan Asset Management	AU$19.2M	Sydney-based online fashion retailer The Iconic has landed almost $20 million in funding from JP Morgan Asset Management.

1. Internet

Year	Target	Buyer	Value (AU)	Details
2012	Delivery Hero Holding	Kite Ventures	AU$50M	The parent company of Delivery Hero Australia has raised $50 million in an investment round led by Kite Ventures, less than a year after the global food delivery service launched locally.
2012	Jump On It	Living Social	AU$40M	Living Social has acquired the remainder of shares in Jump On It, following its minority investment stake in 2011.
2012	Ganji.com	Macquarie Group Limited	US$15M	Ganji.com, a Beijing-based privately held online classified services provider raised a significant amount of capital from investors.
2012	Pinion	Microsoft's Bing Fund	N/A	Australian gaming start-up Pinion has been selected as one of the first companies to participate in Microsoft's new Bing Fund, which is an angel investment incubator led by VoodooPC founder Rahul Sood.
2012	bestrecipes.com.au	News Limited	N/A	News Limited has acquired user-created food recipe website bestrecipes.com.au for an undisclosed sum.
2012	DTDigital Pty Limited	Ogilvy & Mather	N/A	Ogilvy & Mather acquired a 33.3% stake in DTDigital (web design and website development services).
2012	Eatability Pty Limited	Optus Mobile Pty Limited	AU$6M	Optus has acquired Eatability.com, which is a restaurant review website that started up in 2003.
2012	Deals.com.au	Ouffer.com	N/A	Ouffer Australia and deals.com.au, both online retail businesses, have agreed to merge creating Australia's sixth largest purely online business.
2012	Buyin-vite.com.au	Ozsale.com.au	N/A	Ozsale.com.au, an invitation-only online shopping website, has acquired flash sale competitor Buyin-vite.com.au.

1. Internet

Year	Target	Buyer	Value (AU)	Details
2012	Kondoot	Preliminary public offering	AU$10M	Kondoot has lodged a prospectus with ASIC for the preliminary public offering of its shares to raise investment "for the purposes of marketing and expansion".
2012	Red Bubble	Private investors	AU$7M	Headed by former Looksmart senior vice-president Martin Hosking as chief executive, Red Bubble is an online community of artists whose work can be printed onto a T-shirt, poster or any number of products for a small fee and delivered to customers' doors. Redbubble raised AU$7M from private investors. Early-stage investors include former Realestate.com.au CEO, Simon Baker, Bebo founder Michael Birch and former Morgan Stanley Australia MD Richard Cawsey.
2012	Shippin-gEasy.com	Private Investors	AU$2M	ShippingEasy, an online shipping company, has received a large investment from private investors. Launched in 2011, ShippingEasy.com provides SMEs with a real-time multi-channel platform where domestic and international shipping needs across multiple online and offline retail stores can be managed through a retailer's eCommerce platform or aggregated through the ShippingEasy.com dashboard.
2012	Brasil Online and OCC	SEEK	N/A	SEEK has entered into agreements to increase its ownership stakes in Brasil Online and OCC. Brasil Online operates two leading employment websites (including the market leader Catho Online) in Brazil and OCC is the leading employment website in Mexico. On completion of the acquisitions, SEEK's shareholding will increase from 30% to 51% in Brasil Online and 41% to 57% in OCC with SEEK now holding controlling interests across both businesses.
2012	StyleTread	Starfish Ventures	AU$12M	Starfish Ventures has joined existing investors Lakestar, Nine Entertainment Co., and Adinvest to participate in the Company's Series C financing.

1. Internet

Year	Target	Buyer	Value (AU)	Details
2012	Styletread	Starfish Ventures, Lakestar, Nine Entertainment, Adinvest	AU$12M	Starfish joins existing investors, Lakestar, Adinvest and Nine Entertainment in a Series C round for the online shoe retailer.
2012	Ooyala	Telstra	$35M	Telstra has invested $35m in Ooyala, a US-based IPTV video company. The two companies are working on a commercial agreement that will see Telstra deploy Ooyala's software and analytics into its IPTV platform, T-Box.
2012	Dimmi	Telstra	N/A	Telstra's Applications and Ventures Group, in partnership with Village, signed off on an investment in Dimmi, the real-time online restaurants reservations website.
2012	Adam Internet Pty Ltd.	Telstra Corporation Limited	$48.6M	Telstra has agreed to acquire Adam Internet Pty Ltd, an Australia-based internet service provider. The transaction is in line with Telstra's strategy to expand its customer base and enhance its business. The transaction will also enable Adam Internet to expand nationally.
2012	AutoBase Limited	Trade Me Group Limited	N/A	Trade Me, the NZ based auction and classifieds website, has purchased the vehicle listing aggregator, AutoBase Limited.
2012	Adam lockers	TZ Limited and Temando	N/A	TZ Limited has struck a deal with one of Australia's largest e-commerce delivery companies, Temando, to deliver parcels to the network of Adam lockers, which can be accessed 24 hours a day.

2. Telecommunications deals

Year	Target	Buyer	Value	Details
2015	Applaud IT	BigAir	AU$1.2M	BigAir a telecommunications provider has acquired Australian based managed services specialist Applaud IT.
2015	NewSat	SpeedCast International	AU$12M	SpeedCast International has acquired NewSat's Perth and Adelaide teleports as well as its satellite business.
2015	Spirit Telecom (Australia) Pty Ltd	Arunta Resources Limited	AU$12M	Arunta Resources, the Australian company engaged in mineral exploration has acquired Spirit Telecom an Australian provider of broadband services.
2015	Amcom	Vocus	$1.2B	Vocus has announced its intention to acquire Amcom. The deal is still pending court approval and regulatory sign-offs.
2015	Crown Castle Australia Pty Ltd	UniSuper and others	AU$2B	Crown Castle Australia, the Australian company that operates telecommunications towers has been acquired by UniSuper and others.
2015	AFC Group Pty Ltd	AFC Telecommunications LLC	N/A	AFL Telecommunications, a US based company that manufactures and installs fibre optic cables has acquired AFC Group an Australian based company that also manufactures and installs fibre optic cables.
2015	Call Plus	M2	AU$245M	Australian based M2 is set to acquire New Zealand's third largest ISP Call Plus.
2015	Telcom New Zealand International	MyNetFone	NZ22.4M	MyNetFone, the Australian-based telecommunications provider, has acquired Telcom New Zealand International's global wholesale voice business.
2015	Macquarie Telecom	Vocus	$15.6M	Vocus has acquired a 14.5% stake in Macquarie Telecom in a move that Vocus hopes will lead to a closer relationship between the two companies.

2. Telecommunications

Year	Target	Buyer	Value	Details
2015	Enterprise Data Corp (Data Centre Business)	Vocus Communications Limited	$24M	Vocus Communications, the Australian data network provider, has acquired the Melbourne and Sydney data centres previously owned by Enterprise Data Corp.
2014	Megaport	Amcom	$15M	Megaport has sold its fibre assets on the east coast of Australia to Amcom for AU$15M.
2014	Questek Australia Pty Ltd	Hills Holdings Limited	N/A	Hills Limited, Australia-based investment company engaged in lifestyle and sustainability, electronics and communications, and building and industrial businesses activities, has acquired Questek Australia Pty Ltd, the Australia-based company engaged in designing, manufacturing and supplying of nurse call and communication systems to healthcare providers.
2014	Tech2 Group	iiNet	N/A	iiNet has acquired a 60% stake in Tech2 Group. Tech2 Group is a provider of technical services and iiNet is looking to use this experience in its provision of NBN services to residential and business customers.
2014	Orion Satellite Systems Pty Limited	IPSTAR Australia Pty Ltd	AU$13M	IPSTAR Australia Pty Ltd, an Australian-based satellite operator has acquired Orion Satellite Systems Pty Limited, an Australian based company that provides telecommunications services.
2014	Ozefax Pty Limited and Betteroff Networks Pty ltd	j2 Global Communications Inc	N/A	j2 Global Communications, Inc., a US-based provider of messaging and communication services has acquired Ozefax Pty Limited, an Australian based provider of online fax and support services and Betteroff Networks Pty Ltd, an Australian-based provider of online fax and support services.
2014	iBoss	MyNetFone	AU$1.4M	Following the collapse of ispONE, iBoss, the software platform that links wholesale telco operators with their suppliers and manages billing, communications and other operations have been sold to MyNetFone.

2. Telecommunications

Year	Target	Buyer	Value	Details
2014	SingTel Optus Pty Limited (Hybrid Coaxial Network)	NBN Co Limited	N/A	NBN Co Limited has acquired hybrid coaxial networks from SingTel Optus Pty Limited.
2014	Telstra Corporation Limited (Copper and Hybrid Fibre Coaxial Networks)	NBN Co Limited	N/A	NBN Co Limited has acquired copper and hybrid fibre-coaxial cable networks from Telstra Corporation.
2014	Sensis Pty Ltd	Platinum Equity, LLC	AU$454M	Telstra has sold 70% of Sensis to the Californian private equity fund Platinum Equity.
2014	Telstra Corporation Limited (certain assets) and PT Telekomunikasi Indonesia Tbk (certain assets)	PT Telekomunikasi Indonesia Tbk / Telstra Corporation Limited – joint venture	N/A	PT Telekomunikasi Indonesia Tbk listed Indonesia based telecom group and Telstra have entered into a joint venture to provide network application and services products in Indonesia.
2014	Oceanic Broadband	SpeedCast	N/A	SpeedCast, a global satellite telecommunications service provider, has acquired Oceanic Broadband for an undisclosed amount.
2014	Matrixx	Telstra	N/A	Telstra has invested in Matrixx in order to provide its customers with real-time data usage reports.
2014	Nemco	Telstra	N/A	Telstra has invested in Nemco a company that specialises in mass communication.
2014	Pacnet	Telstra	AU$858M	Telstra has acquired the Asian telecommunications and services provider Pacnet for AU$858M.

2. Telecommunications

Year	Target	Buyer	Value	Details
2014	SNP	Telstra	AU$50M	Telstra has entered into a joint venture with security firm SNP for the purpose of establishing a platform in the monitored security industry. The joint venture is to be named TelstraSNP Monitoring.
2014	TeleSign	Telstra	N/A	Telstra has made an investment in US-based mobile phone authentication services provider TeleSign.
2014	O2 Networks	Telstra	AU$40M	Telstra's acquisition of network integrator O2 Networks adds to Telstra's network applications and services division, enhancing Telstra's ability to provide data centre and cloud services.
2014	iBoss and One Telecom	Vocus	AU$500K	Telecommunications provider Vocus has purchased the customer bases of iBoss and OneTelecom after both companies entered administration.
2014	FX Networks	Vocus Communications	AU$107M	Vocus has acquired New Zealand fibre optic network provider FX Networks.
2013	aCure Technology Pty Ltd	Amcom Telecommunications Limited	AU$14M	Amcom Telecommunications, an Australia-based provider of data connectivity and telecommunication services, has acquired aCure Technology an Australian company providing IT support and consulting services.
2013	Optimal Cable Services Pty Ltd	America Fujikura Ltd	N/A	America Fujikura Ltd, the US-based company that is engaged in manufacturing, engineering and installing fibre optic products and equipment and a subsidiary of Fujikura Ltd, the listed Japanese based electric wire and cables manufacturer, has acquired Optimal Cable Services Pty Ltd, the Australia-based company that manufactures and supplies fibre optic cable and connectivity products, for an undisclosed amount.

2. Telecommunications

Year	Target	Buyer	Value	Details
2013	Mnet Group Limited	Ansible Mobile Pty Limited	AU$5.5M	Mnet Group, a mobile content and mobile marketing services provider, has completed the transaction with Ansible to sell its stake in Mercury Mobility (Australia) Pty Ltd, Mnet Corporation Pty Ltd and certain assets of Mnet North America Inc, the US-based holding company having interest in companies engaged in providing wireless internet services and applications and mobile marketing.
2013	Intelligent IP Communications Pty Ltd	BigAir Group Limited	$20M	BigAir Group, an Australia-based business engaged in providing wireless broadband services, has acquired Intelligent IP Communications, an Australia-based company engaged in the provision of IP telephony, video conferencing and internet services to businesses.
2013	Progility Pty Ltd	ILX Group Plc	$27M	ILX Group, a UK-based company, engaged in delivering business training and educational products has acquired Progility an Australia-based company engaged in providing communication systems integration services.
2013	Eftel Limited	M2 Telecommunications Group Limited	$38.5M	Melbourne-based telecommunications services company M2 Telecommunications Group has acquired Eftel Limited, an Australian internet service provider, after also buying Dodo Australia Pty Ltd.
2013	Dodo Australia Pty Ltd	M2 Telecommunications Group Limited	$203.9M	M2 Telecommunications Group Limited has acquired Dodo Australia Pty Ltd. The transaction will provide M2 with a consumer telecom business complementing its existing consumer division.
2013	mia Pty Ltd	Mandalay Digital Group, Inc	$7M	Mandalay, a US company that provides mobile services enabling mobile content distribution, has acquired mia Pty Ltd, an Australia-based provider of mobile solutions to enable experiences on connected devices.

2. Telecommunications

Year	Target	Buyer	Value	Details
2013	PennyTel and iVoiSys	MyNetFone	N/A	MyNetFone received court approval to take over the customer bases of two Sydney-based voice-over-IP resellers which went into liquidation amid allegations of fraud. MyNetFone negotiated with the liquidators of PennyTel and iVoiSys to take over the assets of both companies, which equates to approximately 200,000 customers.
2013	Nextgen Networks Pty Ltd; Metronode Pty Ltd; Infoplex Pty Ltd	Ontario Teachers' Pension Plan	$619.5M	Ontario Teachers' Pension Plan, a Canada-based pension fund engaged in managing equity, fixed income and alternative investment portfolios, has agreed to acquire a 70% stake in Nextgen Networks Pty Ltd, Metronode Pty Ltd., and Infoplex Pty Ltd. Nextgen Networks, Metronode and Infoplex together comprise of 70% of Leighton Holding's overall telecommunications business.
2013	NSC Group Pty Ltd	Telstra Corporation Limited	$50M	Telstra has acquired NSC Group Pty Ltd, an Australia-based provider of unified communications, network infrastructure and contact centre solutions.
2013	AAPT	TPG	$450M	TPG has acquired AAPT after the previous owner Telecom NZ put the company for sale in October 2013, having initially acquired AAPT in 2000 for $2.3 billion.
2012	NEC Australia's Nextep	AAPT	N/A	Australia's business telecommunications infrastructure company AAPT will purchase NEC Australia's Nextep DSL business as part of a long-term strategic Alliance between the two organisations. Nextep is a wholesale carriage service provider delivering broadband services to urban, metropolitan and regional areas.
2012	TR Hirecom	Communications Australia Pty Limited	N/A	Communications Australia, the Australia-based systems integrator specialising in unified communications and contact centres, has acquired TR Hirecom, the Australia-based two-way radio communications rental company.

2. Telecommunications

Year	Target	Buyer	Value	Details
2012	Codan Limited	CPI International Holding Corp	US$9M	Codan Limited has reached agreement to sell its satellite communications assets to CPI International Holding Corp and its wholly-owned subsidiary CPI International, Inc.
2012	iiNet	Crown Castle Australia	N/A	Crown Castle Australia will acquire the network of radio towers in South Australia built by Internode subsidiary Agile Communications. The network is owned by iiNet, which also acquired Internode.
2012	Engin Pty Limited	Eftel Limited	$9.1M	Eftel Limited, a listed Australia-based provider of broadband, wireless broadband, mobile, home phone services, has agreed to acquire Engin Pty Limited, which is an Australia-based broadband telecommunication provider.
2012	C4i Pty Ltd	Exelis Inc	$16M	Exelis Inc has agreed to acquire C4i Pty Ltd from Longreach Group Limited. Exelis Inc, a US-based company, provides defence and information solutions to global military, government and commercial customers. C4i Pty Ltd, an Australia-based company, provides designing, manufacturing and integrating communications solutions to defence, public safety, utilities, transport, and oil and gas markets.
2012	AMT Group	Glentel Inc	AU$70.6M	Canada's Glentel Inc has bought an 83% stake in telecommunications retailer AMT Group, which operates and manages over 210 stores nationally across Australia under Allphones and Virgin Mobile branding.
2012	Internode	iiNet Ltd	AU$104M	iiNet has acquired Aguile Pty Ltd and Internode Pty Ltd, both of which are internet and telephone services companies.

2. Telecommunications

Year	Target	Buyer	Value	Details
2012	Message Stick Communications Pty Ltd	Indigenous Business Australia	N/A	Indigenous Business Australia has acquired 31% stake in Message Stick Communications Pty Ltd, the Australia-based provider of communications services, for an undisclosed consideration.
2012	Primus Telecom Australia	M2 Telecommunications Group Limited	AU$192M	M2 Telecommunications Group has acquired Primus Telecom, which is expected to provide M2 access to 165,000 additional consumer contacts and the iPrimus and Primus brands and network.
2012	biNu	Private investors	US$2M	Heavyweight investors including Google executive chairman Eric Schmidt and the co-founder of Seek.com.au, Paul Bassat, have invested $2 million in biNu, an Australian mobile app platform targeting people who do not have access to smartphones.
2012	Vividwireless Group Ltd	Singtel Optus Pty Ltd	AU$230M	Singtel Optus acquired Vividwireless, an Australia-based wireless broadband and internet services company.
2012	Time Telecom Pty ltd	Southern Cross Telco Pty Ltd	AU$18.35M	Southern Cross Telco, a subsidiary of M2 Telecommunications, has acquired Time Telecom, which is a telecommunications service provider.
2012	Australian Satellite Communications	SpeedCast	N/A	Hong Kong networks company, SpeedCast has acquired satellite company, Australian Satellite Communications.
2012	Pactel International Pty Ltd	SpeedCast Ltd	AU$27.5M	SpeedCast, a Hong Kong-based company, engaged in providing satellite communication services has acquired Pactel, an Australia-based company providing satellite equipment.
2012	Ipera Communications	Vocus Communications	AU$9.8M	Vocus Communications has entered a binding agreement to acquire Newcastle-based data centre and fibre provider Ipera Communications.
2012	TelstraClear Ltd	Vodafone New Zealand	US$390M	Vodafone has acquired Telstra Corporation's NZ subsidiary.

3. Media & content deals

Year	Target	Buyer	Value	Details
2015	Hoyts Corporation	Wanda Cinema Line	AU$1B	Hoyts Corporation the Australian cinema operator has been acquired by Wanda a Chinese cinema operator.
2015	Match Media	Publicis Groupe SA	N/A	Publicis Groupe a French based company that provides marketing solutions has acquired Match Media an Australian based company that also provides marketing solutions.
2015	Nine Live	Affinity Equity Partners	AU$640M	Nine Entertainment has sold Nine Live, which includes Ticketek, to private equity firm Affinity Equity Partners.
2015	Beautyheaven Group	Bauer Media	N/A	Bauer Media has acquired Beautyheaven Group, a provider of information services regarding beauty products and homes.
2015	Belgiovane Williams Mackay Pty Ltd	Dentsu Aegis Network Limited	N/A	Dentsu Aegis Network Limited, a UK based branding and marketing company has acquired a 51% stake in Australian advertising company Belgiovane Williams Mackay Pty Ltd.
2015	Metro Media Publishing Holdings	Fairfax Media	AU$72M	Fairfax Media, which already owned 50% of Metro Media Publishing Holdings has acquired the remaining 50% of Metro Media Publishing Holdings. Metro Media Publishing Holdings owns Melbourne property portal reviewproperty.com.au, as well as several newspapers.
2015	Pedestrian Group Pty Ltd	Mi9	AU$11M	Mi9, a subsidiary of Nine Entertainment Co. and an Australian based company that provides online media services has acquired a majority stake in Pedestrian Group, an Australian online publishing company.
2015	Globecast Australia	Telstra	N/A	Telstra has acquired Globecast Australia a provider of media services for broadcasters in Australia for an undisclosed sum.

3. Media & Content

Year	Target	Buyer	Value	Details
2014	Reactive Media	Accenture Plc	N/A	Accenture Plc, the Ireland-based technology consulting company has acquired Reactive Media, an Australian based company specialising in the provision of digital marketing.
2014	Adconion Pty Limited	Amobee Group Pte. Ltd	AU$250M	Amobee Group Pte Ltd, the Singapore-based investment holding company, has acquired Adconion Pty Limited, Australian-based company engaged in advertising solutions.
2014	96FM	APN News & Media Limited	AU$78M	APN News & Media Limited, the listed Australian media company, has acquired 96FM a Perth radio station.
2014	Buspak Advertising (Hong Kong) Limited	APN News & Media Limited	AU$14M	APN News & Media Limited has acquired full ownership of Buspak Advertising (Hong Kong).
2014	The Radio Network and Australian Radio Network Pty Ltd	APN News and Media Limited	AU$247M	APN News and Media Limited, an Australian-based media company has acquired a 50% stake in Australian Radio Network Pty Ltd an Australian based operator of radio stations and the Radio Network, a New Zealand based radio operator.
2014	Audio Network Australia Pty Ltd	Audio Network	N/A	Audio network has acquired 49% of the shareholding in Audio Network Australia Pty Ltd, enabling the Australian subsidiary to become a fully integrated part of the Audio Network Group.

3. Media & Content

Year	Target	Buyer	Value	Details
2014	The Intelligent Investor Publishing Pty Ltd	Australasian Wealth Investments Limited	AU$6.9M	Australasian Wealth Investments Limited, the listed Australia-based investment holding company engaged in providing wealth management products and services and having interest in companies in the thematics, digital distribution, research & information and funds management industry, has agreed to acquire The Intelligent Investor Publishing Pty Ltd, the Australia-based subscription based equity research firm.
2014	GoConnect Limited	Centurion Investments Services Pty Ltd	US$13M	Centurion Investments Services Pty Ltd, an Australian-based investment holding company has acquired GoConnect Limited an Australian based online media communications and software company.
2014	HWW Ltd	Gracenote, Inc	AU$22M	Gracenote, Inc the United States based digital media company has acquired HWW Ltd an Australian based company that specialises in publishing lifestyle and entertainment content.
2014	The Hoyts Corporation Pty Ltd	ID Leisure International Capital	AU$900M	ID Leisure International Capital, the Australian based but British Virgin Island incorporated investment fund of Mr. Sun Xishuang, a Chinese private investor, has acquired the Hoyts Corporation, an Australian company operating movie cinemas.
2014	Arte Mobile Technology	iSentric Limited	AU$18M	iSentric has acquired Arte Mobile Technology for the distribution of mobile content in Indonesia.

3. Media & Content

Year	Target	Buyer	Value	Details
2014	Fairfax Radio Network Pty Ltd	Macquarie Radio Network Limited	AU$141M	Macquarie Radio Network Limited has acquired Fairfax Radio Network Pty Ltd.
2014	Funtastic Limited (Madman group companies)	Madman Film and Media Pty Ltd	AU$21.5M	Funtastic has sold the Madman group companies to Madman Film and Media Pty Ltd.
2014	The Performance Factory	Mobile Embrace Limited	AU$7M	Mobile Embrace, the Australian mobile marketing company, has acquired The Performance Factory, another Australian-based mobile marketing company.
2014	Silk Studios	NEP Australia	N/A	NEP Australia, an Australian broadcaster, has acquired Silk Studios, an Australian-based production company.
2014	Quikflix	Nine Entertainment	AU$1M	Nine Entertainment has purchased a minority stake in Quikflix in the form of redeemable preference shares.
2014	Morrison Media	Pacific Star Network Limited	AU$11M	Pacific Star Network, the Australian based radio broadcasting company has acquired Morrison Media, the lifestyle and sports publishing company.
2014	Active Display Group	STW Communications Group Ltd	AU$43M	STW Communications Group Ltd, an Australian-based marketing services company has acquired Active Display Group an Australian based company that designs and manufacturers retail marketing campaigns.
2013	Oddfellows Pty Ltd	Aegis Media Australia	N/A	Aegis Media Australia, the Australian-based company, engaged in providing advertising and media services, has acquired a 51% stake in Oddfellows Pty Ltd, the Australian-based company engaged in advertising.

3. Media & Content

Year	Target	Buyer	Value(AU)	Details
2013	Volt Media	Alphabird	N/A	Alphabird, a leading global digital publishing solutions company, headquartered in San Francisco, announced the acquisition of Volt Media, one of the largest independent premium video advertising and technology companies in Australia and New Zealand.
2013	iNC Digital Media	APN News and Media Limited	$9M	APN News and Media Limited, Australia-based media company, has acquired iNC Digital Media, Australia-based provider of online retail advertising and digital distribution services, this acquisition will help APN News broaden the range of digital products for sectors such as travel, finance, motoring and real estate.
2013	Sunshine Coast Broadcasters Pty Ltd	Eon Broadcasting Pty Ltd	$17.75M	Eon Broadcasting has agreed to purchase Sea FM and Mix FM from Sunshine Coast Broadcasters, following a breach by Sunshine where it had exceeded the permitted number of commercial FM radio licences.
2013	Netus	Fairfax Media Limited	N/A	Fairfax Media Limited has acquired Netus, the Australia-based technology investment company.
2013	nextmedia Pty Ltd	Forum Media Group GmbH	N/A	Forum Media Group GmbH, a Germany based company which through its subsidiaries focuses on information, education, and entertainment businesses, has acquired nextmedia Pty Ltd, an Australia-based company engaged in publishing magazines.
2013	Brand New Media Pty Ltd	HighPoint Capital Pty Ltd	N/A	HighPoint Capital Pty Ltd, Australia-based private equity firm has acquired a significant minority stake in Brand New Media Pty Ltd, an Australia-based media and integrated communications company.
2013	Merlon Health Communications Pty Ltd	Hills Holdings Limited	N/A	Hills Holdings, an Australia-based company engaged in providing electronics and communication services has acquired Merlon Health Communications, an Australia-based producer and provider of nurse call and patient entertainment solutions for the healthcare industry.

3. Media & Content

Year	Target	Buyer	Value	Details
2013	eBUS Limited	Independent Media Distribution Plc	N/A	Independent Media Distribution Plc, provider of content distribution and advertising services to broadcasters, media agencies and production houses, has acquired eBUS Limited, the Singapore-based digital advertising firm.
2013	Global Television Limited	NEP Broadcasting, LLC	N/A	NEP Broadcasting, LLC, the US-based provider of outsourced television production services has acquired Global Television Limited, the Australian-based company engaged in live television broadcasts and studio productions.
2013	Ninemsn Pty Limited	Nine Entertainment Co	AU$41M	Nine Entertainment, the Australia-based media and entertainment company engaged in television, magazine and digital businesses, has agreed to acquire a 50% stake in Ninemsn Pty Limited, the Australia-based online media company providing MSN online services with TV and magazine brands, from Microsoft Corporation, the listed US based company engaged in developing, licensing and supporting a range of software products and services.
2013	WIN Corporation Pty Ltd (Adelaide television station)	Nine Entertainment Co	AU$140M	Nine Entertainment Co has agreed to purchase WIN Corporation's Adelaide television station.
2013	One Africa Media	SEEK Limited	US$20M	SEEK Limited has acquired a 25% stake in One Africa Media in order to capture the large market opportunities across Africa.
2013	Australian Local Search Pty Ltd	Sensis Pty Ltd	N/A	Sensis Pty Ltd has acquired Australian Local Search Pty Ltd, the Australia-based company engaged in operating online directory of Australian businesses, from News Limited.

3. Media & Content

Year	Target	Buyer	Value	Details
2013	Australian Associated Press Pty Ltd	Sentia Media Pty Ltd	N/A	Sentia Media Pty Ltd, an Australia-based provider of media information, analysis and advice, has agreed to acquire the Australia and New Zealand-based media monitoring business Australian Associated Press Pty Ltd.
2013	Totem Industries Pty Ltd; The Totem Onelove Group Pty Ltd	SFX Entertainment Inc	AU$75M	SFX Entertainment Inc, the US-based company engaged in broadcasting and managing live shows, has agreed to acquire The Totem Onelove Group Pty Ltd, the Australia based music event company and Totem Industries Pty Ltd, the Australia-based provider of public relation counselling services.
2012	ViDM Pty Ltd	AlphaBird, Inc	AU$16M	AlphaBird, Inc, the US-based company that provides social video engagement solutions, has acquired ViDM Pty Ltd, the Australia-based company engaged in providing digital media and advertising technology solutions.
2012	Chomp	Apple Inc	US$50M	Apple has acquired the mobile app search engine Chomp. Chomp was created by Australian-born internet entrepreneurs Ben Keighran and Cathy Edwards.
2012	Screentime Pty Ltd	Banijay Entertainment SAS	N/A	Banijay Entertainment SAS, France-based company engaged in the production and distribution of online, ad-funded, and branded entertainment content, has acquired majority stake in Screentime Pty Ltd, the Australia-based company that offers film and television production and distribution services.
2012	ACP Magazines Ltd	Bauer Media Group	AU$500M	Bauer Media Group, Germany based magazine publishing company, has agreed to acquire ACP Magazines, an Australia-based magazine and digital content publishing company.
2012	Q Ltd	Beyond International Ltd	AU$3.25M	Beyond International, the TV production and distribution company behind Mythbusters, has acquired digital marketing group Q Ltd.

3. Media & Content

Year	Target	Buyer	Value	Details
2012	Purple Communications	Cannings/Cannings Purple	AU$8M	Cannings Corporate Communications, the Australia-based PR firm, has acquired 49% stake in Purple Communications, the Australia-based public relation company.
2012	Reed Business Information	Catalyst Investment Managers Pty Ltd	AU$30M	Catalyst, an Australia-based equity firm, has acquired Reed Business Information, an Australia-based business that offers hard and soft copy business news and information products.
2012	Sky Network Television Limited	Credit Suisse Investments (Australia) Limited	US$179.4M	Credit Suisse Investments (Australia) Limited has agreed to acquire an 11.11% stake in Sky Network Television Limited, a New Zealand-based provider of multi-channel, pay television and free-to-air television services.
2012	Viva9 Pty Ltd	Digital Performance Group Ltd	US$2M	Digital Performance Group Ltd, an ASX listed holding company for performance-based digital marketing, has agreed to acquire Viva9 Pty Ltd, Australia's second largest affiliate network. Digital Performance Group intends to merge its own affiliate marketing company, dgm, with Viva9.
2012	Hi-5 Operations Pty Limited	Dragonrider Opportunity Fund II LP	N/A	Dragonrider Opportunity Fund II LP, the Singapore-based private equity fund has acquired Hi-5 Operations Pty Limited, the Australia-based pre-school television show.
2012	Metro Media Publishing	Fairfax Media	AU$35M	The ACCC has approved Fairfax Media's 50% merger with Metro Media Publishing (publisher of Melbourne real estate advertising paper The Weekly Review). The new entity is valued at around $125 million.
2012	Austar United Communications	Foxtel	AU$2B	Foxtel, the pay-TV operator, has acquired Austar, another pay-TV provider after making court-enforceable undertakings to the ACCC.

3. Media & Content

Year	Target	Buyer	Value	Details
2012	The Premium Movie Partnership	Foxtel Management Pty Ltd	AU$15M	Foxtel Management Pty Ltd, the Australia-based company, engaged in providing pay television services, has acquired Australia-based assets of The Premium Movie Partnership, which is a company engaged in providing cable and other pay television services.
2012	DMG Radio Australia Pty Ltd	Illyria Pty Ltd	AU$100M	Illyria Pty Ltd, the Australia-based investment holding company, has acquired 50% stake of DMG Radio Australia Pty Ltd, an Australia-based company that owns and operates radio stations.
2012	Hyro Limited	KIT Digital, Inc	AU$17M	KIT Digital, Inc, provider of internet software products and solutions that enable customers to distribute video content through internet websites and mobile devices, has acquired Hyro Limited's Thailand and Australian operations to strengthen its digital's service offering in Australia and the Asia-Pacific region.
2012	GEON Group	Kohlberg Kravis Roberts & Co LP; Allegro Private Equity	N/A	Allegro Private Equity, the Australia-based private equity firm and Kohlberg Kravis Roberts & Co LP, the US-based private equity firm, have acquired GEON Group, the Australia-based printing company.
2012	Sports Marketing & Management Pty Ltd	Lagardere Unlimited Australia Pty Ltd	N/A	Lagardere Unlimited Australia Pty Ltd, the Australia-based sports marketing and management company, has acquired Sports Marketing & Management Pty Ltd, the Australia-based company engaged in the provision of sports marketing and management services.
2012	Live Nation Australasia	Live Nation Entertainment, Inc	AU$35M	Live Nation Entertainment, Inc, the US-based producer and promoter of live music concerts and tours, has acquired Michael Coppel Presents, the Australia-based company engaged in the promotion of concerts.

3. Media & Content

Year	Target	Buyer	Value	Details
2012	5th Finger	Merkle	N/A	Merkle, a leading customer relationship marketing firm and the largest privately-held agency in the US, has acquired 5th Finger, a leading technology-enabled mobile solutions provider.
2012	zeebox Ltd	Network Ten Pty Ltd	N/A	Network Ten and UK company zeebox Ltd will enter into a joint venture to launch zeebox's award-winning app on the local market. Zeebox uniquely provides consumers with a comprehensive social TV discovery and interaction service, while enabling broadcasters and brands to engage with TV fans across all channels.
2012	Australian Independent Business Media	News Limited	AU$30M	News Limited announced acquisition of parent company of Business Spectator and Eureka Report, Australian Independent Business Media, to boost digital revenues for $30M cash.
2012	Venuemob	Optus-Innov8 Seed	AU$450K	Venuemob is a recipient of the Optus-Innov8 Seed Program. Venuemob is an information and booking service for a hand-picked selection of bars, restaurants, reception centres, and function rooms in Melbourne.
2012	121cast	Optus-Innov8 Seed	AU$250K	121cast is a recipient of the Optus-Innov8 Seed Program. 121cast is the Melbourne-based start-up behind SoundGecko, a service that converts text into spoken words.
2012	Eye Corp Pty Ltd	Outdoor Media Operations Pty Limited	AU$113M	Outdoor Media Operations, the Australia-based acquisition vehicle formed by Champ Private Equity, the Australia-based private equity firm, has agreed to acquire Eye Corp Pty Ltd, the Australia-based company engaged in the provision of multi-format advertising solutions.
2012	APN Outdoor Pty Limited	Quadrant Private Equity Pty Limited	AU$136M	Quadrant Private Equity Pty Limited, the Australia-based private equity firm has agreed to acquire a 50% stake in APN Outdoor Pty Limited, the Australia-based outdoor advertising company.

3. Media & Content

Year	Target	Buyer	Value	Details
2012	Belgiovane Williams Mackay Pty Ltd	Rob Belgiovane (Private Investor); Paul Williams (Private Investor); Jamie Mackay (Private Investor)	AU$7.5M	Rob Belgiovane, Jamie Mackay and Paul Williams, the Australia-based private individuals having interest in the advertising sector, have acquired 51% stake in Belgiovane Williams Mackay Pty Ltd, the Australia-based advertising agency.
2012	BuzzNumbers	Sentia Media	N/A	BuzzNumbers, a social media tracking start-up launched by prominent tech scene figure Nick Holmes a Court, has been purchased by Sentia Media.
2012	Pixable	Singapore Telecommunications	US$26.5M	Singapore Telecommunications has acquired New York-based startup Pixable for $US26.5 million. Pixable is known for its smartphone app that prioritises photos on social networks for consumers.
2012	Amobee	Singapore Telecommunications Ltd	US$321M	Singtel has acquired Amobee, a Silicon Valley start-up in the mobile advertising sector on undisclosed terms.
2012	Hoyts Distribution Pty Ltd	StudioCanal SA	AU$25M	StudioCanal SA, the France-based company, engaged in the production, co-production, acquisition and distribution of movies has agreed to acquire Hoyts Distribution Pty Ltd, the Australia-based company engaged in film distribution.
2012	Switched on Media	STW	N/A	Marketing and communications group STW has taken a majority share in Sydney based Switched on Media, which specialises in search engine optimisation, pay-per-click advertising, digital content and social media.

3. Media & Content

Year	Target	Buyer	Value	Details
2012	Amblique Pty Ltd; Markitforce; Maverick Marketing and Communications; Switched on Media	STW Communications Group Ltd	AU$30.6M	STW Communications Group Ltd, the listed Australia-based marketing services company engaged in offering advertising and diversified communications services has acquired: • 75% of Markitforce Pty Ltd; • 80% of Maverick Marketing and Communications Pty Ltd; • 75% of Switched On Media Pty Ltd and • 40% of Amblique.
2012	Buchanan Group Pty Ltd	STW Communications Group Ltd	N/A	STW Communications Group Ltd, the listed Australia-based marketing services company engaged in offering advertising and diversified communications services, has acquired a 60% stake in Buchanan Group Pty Ltd, the Australia-based provider of branded advertising solutions.
2012	Village Roadshow Entertainment Group	Trinity Opportunities Limited	AU$274M	Trinity Opportunities Limited has acquired an undisclosed stake in Village Roadshow Entertainment Group. Trinity Opportunities Limited, the Australia-based investment firm, having interests in companies engaged in movie and music production. Village Roadshow Entertainment Group, the Australia-based company, is engaged in movie and music production.
2012	Australian Independent Business Media Pty Ltd	Twenty-First Century Fox, Inc	AU$25M	News Corporation, the US-based Media Company, publisher of newspapers, magazines, and books and provider of television and cable services, has acquired Australian Independent Business Media Pty Ltd, the Australia-based company engaged in publishing electronic newspaper and journal as well as business websites.
2012	Edge Loyalty Systems	Village Roadshow Limited	N/A	Village Roadshow (listed Australia-based media and entertainment company) has acquired Edge Loyalty Systems (Australia-based designer of rewards cards from retailers).

4. Software & information technology deals

Year	Target	Buyer	Value	Details
2015	Marketplacer	Various	AU$10M	Marketplacer an Australian software firm has raised AU$10M from various investors including David Paradice.
2015	Enepath	Telstra	N/A	Telstra has made an investment into Singapore based Enepath a provider of voice technology for the financial services sector.
2015	Torque Data	Virgin Australia Group	N/A	Virgin Australia Group's Velocity Frequent Flyer has acquired Torque Data an Australia leader in data analytics.
2015	Recall Holdings Limited	Iron Mountain Incorporated	AU$3.16B	Iron Mountain the US based information management services company has acquired Recall Holdings a US based but ASX listed company that provides similar services.
2015	Innergi	Iress Limited	N/A	Iress Limited the Australian based provider of technology solutions to financial service providers has acquired Innergi an Australian based online financial knowledge centre
2015	Neto E-commerce Solutions Pty Ltd	Telstra Corporation Limited	N/A	Telstra has acquired an undisclosed stake in Neto E-commerce Solutions an Australian based provider of cloud based e-commerce solutions.
2015	Sportstec Limited	Agile Sports Technologies, Inc	N/A	Sportstec an Australian based company that develops sports analysis software has been acquired by Agile Sports Technologies a US based company that develops coaching tools for sports.
2015	Clipp	Mobile Embrace	AU$4.69M	Clipp, an Australian company that provides a cashless option to purchase drinks and other items from bars and clubs has received a $4.69M investment from Mobile Embrace giving it a 31% stake.

4. Software & information technology

Year	Target	Buyer	Value	Details
2015	Technology Effect and Breeze	Montech Holdings	N/A	Montech Holdings has acquired Technology Effect and Breeze two cloud service providers.
2015	Dataweave	Deloitte	N/A	Deloitte has acquired Australian based Dataweave a company that has a strong presence providing Oracle and other information technology solutions to the public sector.
2015	Megabus Pty Ltd	Friedman Corporation	N/A	Friedman Corporation, a US based company that provides software solutions has acquired Megabus an Australian based company that provides software solutions.
2015	Symplicit Pty Ltd	DWS Advanced Business Solutions Limited	AU$9M	DWS Advanced Business Solutions, an Australian based IT services company has acquired Symplicit an Australian information technology company.
2015	Desktop Mapping Systems Pty Ltd	Technology One Limited	AU$12M	Technology One an Australian based software solutions provider has acquired Desktop Mapping Systems an Australian based company that provides digital mapping.
2015	4impact Group Pty Ltd	Infitecs Pty Ltd	AU$7M	Infitecs, an Australian based analytics company has acquired 4impact Group Pty Ltd an Australian based information technology company.
2015	PJA Solutions Pty Ltd	The Citadel Group Limited	AU$20	The Citadel Group Limited, an Australian based company that provides education in information technology solutions has acquired PJA Solutions an Australian based company that provides software development.

4. Software & information technology

Year	Target	Buyer	Value	Details
2015	Centre for Organisational Innovation (COI)	8Common Limited	N/A	COI, which provides employee surveying, has been acquired by 8CommonGroup, an ASX listed enterprise software company.
2015	TYME (Take Your Money Everywhere)	Commonwealth Bank of Australia	AU$40M	TYME, a South African start-up company that builds and operates digital banking systems that serve customers in emerging marketplaces, has been acquired by the Commonwealth Bank for AU$40M.
2015	C3	Ernst and Young	N/A	EY has acquired C3 an Australian based analytics company that specialises in business intelligence.
2015	ICE Systems	Kloud Solutions	N/A	Kloud Solutions, an Australian based provider of cloud migration services, has acquired a 50% stake in the Australian-based cloud dev-ops and automation consulting firm ICE Systems.
2015	Knowledge Partners Pty Ltd	Konica Minolta Business Solutions Australia Pty Ltd	N/A	Konica Minolta, an Australian based company that provides integrated services has acquired Knowledge Partners, an Australian based company that provides technology that improves business productivity.
2015	First Point Global	KPMG Australia	N/A	KPMG Australia has acquired First Point Global in a move to increase its capabilities in cyber security services.
2015	Dr Foster	Telstra Health	AU$50M	Telstra Health has acquired UK-based health analytics company, Dr Foster. Dr Foster provides healthcare institutions with services that allow them to make better use of their data.

4. Software & information technology

Year	Target	Buyer	Value	Details
2015	My strata Pty Ltd	Urbanise.com Limited	AU$10M	Urbanise.com Limited has acquired Mystrata Pty Ltd, an Australian-based company that provides cloud software used for the management of apartment buildings and commercial towers worldwide.
2014	Wikidocs	Atlassian	N/A	Australian software company Atlassian has acquired Austrian Wikidocs a company that provides software enabling real-time editing of web pages by multiple users.
2014	Doctape	Atlassian	N/A	Doctape, the German based online file management service has been acquired by Australian software company Atlassian.
2014	Oriel Technologies Pty Ltd	BigAir Group Limited	AU$15M	BigAir Group, the Australian-based provider of wireless data services, has acquired Oriel Technologies, an Australian based provider of IT services.
2014	Harbour IT	Canon	N/A	Canon has acquired a majority stake in cloud service provider Harbour IT for an undisclosed sum.
2014	GP Sports	Catapult Sports	N/A	Australian based technology company Catapult Sports which specialises in GPS tracking equipment attached to sports players has acquired GP Sports a direct competitor.
2014	Odecee	Cognizant Technology Solutions Corporation	N/A	Cognizant Technology Solutions, the US-based provider of custom IT development services, has acquired Odecee, the Australian-based provider of mobile and cloud services.
2014	Strategic Payments Services Pty Ltd	Cuscal Limited	AU$37M	Cuscal Limited the Australian based company that provides transactional banking services has acquired Strategic Payments Services Pty Ltd an Australian based company that develops electronic payment processing systems.
2014	Business Access Group	Data#3	AU$6M	Data#3 has acquired Business Access Group, which provides consulting services on strategy, risk and continuity, architecture, and planning

4. Software & information technology

Year	Target	Buyer	Value	Details
2014	Discovery Technology	Data#3	AU$1.5M	Australian based technology services provider Data#3 is set to acquire wi-fi analytics company Discovery Technology.
2014	SmartWard	Datacom	N/A	Datacom, the Australian business technology solution provider, has acquired a 20% stake in SmartWard an Australian health informatics company.
2014	Analytics Group	Deloitte Australia	N/A	Deloitte Australia, the professional services firm, has acquired Canberra based Analytics Group in order to cope with the demand for public sector consultants in the area of IT outsourcing.
2014	Express Data	Dicker Data	N/A	Express Data, a company that specialises in hardware ICT distribution, has been sold to Dicker Data, an Australian based provider of ICT hardware, by Dimension Data.
2014	Oakton	Dimension Data Australia	AU$171M	Dimension Data Australia has moved to buy IT consultancy firm Oakton. Oakton is already a partner of Dimension Data reselling Dimension Data's cloud services since 2013.
2014	DecTech Solutions Pty Ltd	GB Group Plc	AU$37M	GB Group Plc, a listed UK company providing identity intelligence products and services has acquired DecTech Solutions Pty Ltd, an Australian-based decision support company focused on providing credit risk management.
2014	Ezi Holdings Pty Ltd	Global Payments Inc	AU$305M	Global Payments Inc, a US based provider of electronic transaction processing services, has acquired Ezi Holdings an Australian based provider of integrated payment solutions
2014	Enzumo Group of Companies	Goldminex Resources Limited	N/A	Goldminex Resources Limited has acquired the Enzumo Group, an Australian provider of third party software systems and commercial software tools for financial planning.

4. Software & information technology

Year	Target	Buyer	Value	Details
2014	Audio Products Group	Hills Limited	AU$15M	Hills Limited has acquired Audio Products Group, a supplier of professional audio equipment for AU$15M.
2014	Annitel Group Limited	Inabox Group Limited	AU$16M	Telecomunications company Inabox Group Limited has acquired Annitel Group, an Australian IT and cloud provider for AU$16M.
2014	Catapult Sports	Mark Cuban	N/A	Mark Cuban has invested an undisclosed amount to secure an undisclosed amount of Catapult Sports (estimated to be less than 5%). Catapult Sports provides GPS tracking equipment for sports players.
2014	Metaverse Makeovers	Melbourne Angels	AU$750K	Melbourne Angels, an Australian investment group has invested AU$750K into Metaverse Makeovers, an Australian company that designs wearable technology.
2014	Integrators Breeze and Technology Effect	Montech Holdings	AU$29M	Integrators Breeze and Technology Effect, cloud specialists, are set to merge and be acquired by Montech Holdings.
2014	ConvertU2 Technologies and CU2 Global	Motopia Limited	N/A	Motopia Limited, the ASX listed media and technology company, has acquired 49% of ConvertU2 Technologies and 44% of CU2 Global, these companies provide technology that simplifies data management systems.
2014	Pure Hacking	PS&C	AU$16.5M	Australian based cyber security company Pure Hacking has been acquired by PS&C an IT consultancy company for an initial amount of AU$8.3 million, and a potential total of up to AU$16.5 million based on Pure Hackings 2015 financial year performance.

4. Software & information technology

Year	Target	Buyer	Value	Details
2014	Canberra Data Centres Pty Ltd	Quadrant Private Equity Pty Limited	AU$140M	Quadrant Private Equity an Australian based private equity firm has acquired 45% of Canberra Data Centres Pty Ltd an Australian based data centre provider.
2014	Business Records Management LLC	Recall Holdings Limited	AU$77M	Recall Holdings the ASX listed information management solutions company has acquired Business Records Management LLC in the US.
2014	nSynergy	Rhype Limited	AU$25M	Rhype Limited, an Australian based company that distributes software licences has acquired nSynergy a consulting company that specialises in Microsoft licencing.
2014	Stargate Technologies Pty Ltd	Rubik Financial Limited	AU$35M	Rubik Financial Limited, Australian based company that provides cloud-based software to the financial services sector has acquired Stargate Technologies Pty Ltd, an Australian-based company that provides loan processing, customer management platforms and mortgage technology services.
2014	Infinitive Limited	Rubik Financial Limited	AU$17M	Rubik Financial Limited, Australian based company that provides cloud-based software to the financial services sector has acquired Infinitive Limited, an Australian based company that provides e-commerce solutions and digital messaging capabilities to the mortgage industry.
2014	Insight4 Pty Ltd	RXP Services Limited	AU$8M	RXP Services Limited, the Australian based information and communications technology professional services company engaged in consulting has acquired Insight4 Pty Ltd, an Australian-based company that develops software and provides consulting services.

4. Software & information technology

Year	Target	Buyer	Value	Details
2014	Swann Communications Pty Ltd	Shenzhen Infinova Technology Co Ltd	AU$114M	Shenzhen Infinova Technology Co Ltd a Chinese based company that specialises in the production of electronic security products has acquired Swann Communications Pty Ltd an Australian company that also specialises in electronic security equipment.
2014	Leadtec Systems Australia Pty Ltd	SPS Commerce, Inc	AU$17M	SPS Commerce, Inc a United States-based software development company has acquired Leadtec Systems Australia Pty Ltd an Australian based company specialising in business solutions.
2014	IdeaObject	Telstra	N/A	Telstra Health has acquired IdeaObject, an India-based health software developer.
2014	Human Edge Software Corporation Pty Ltd	Tribal Group Plc	AU$15M	Tribal Group Plc, the UK-based provider of consultancy and professional support services to the public sector has acquired Human Edge Software Pty Ltd, an Australian-based provider of student management systems.
2014	Saltbrush Group	UXC Consulting Pty Ltd	N/A	UXC Consulting Pty Ltd the Australian based company that provides IT intelligence services has acquired Saltbrush Group an Australian based company that provides cyber security services.
2014	Neon Stingray Pty Ltd	Valtech	N/A	Valtech, a French consulting group that provides technology solutions has acquired Neon Stingray Pty Ltd an Australian based technology company.
2014	Divvy	Various investors including Blue Chilli	AU$350K	Divvy, a new Australian start-up allowing people to rent out unused carspaces has recently raised $350,000 in funding from various investors including venture technology firm Blue Chilli
2014	Computers Networks Pty Limited	Viatek Services Pty Ltd	N/A	Viatek Services Pty Ltd., the Australian based company providing IT print management services and communications services has acquired Computers Networks Pty Limited, the Australian based company providing business applications and infrastructure consulting solutions.

4. Software & information technology

Year	Target	Buyer	Value	Details
2014	ASG Group's Perth Database	Vocus	AU$11.7M	Vocus has acquired ASG Group's Perth data centre, in addition, Vocus has also picked up the business of ASG Group providing telecommunication services to ASG Group nationally.
2013	Integrated Wireless Pty Ltd	Ascom Holding AG	AU$10M	Ascom Holding AG, the Switzerland-based manufacturer of telecommunications and service automation equipment and systems, has acquired Integrated Wireless Pty Ltd, the Australian-based provider of wireless communication systems and workflow solutions.
2013	WindowLogic	Atos SE	N/A	Atos SE, the listed France-based IT services company offering transactional services, consulting, systems integration, and managed services, has acquired WindowLogic, the Australia-based information management systems and service provider. The acquisition is in line with Atos' growth strategy. The acquisition will enable Atos to expand its geographical and market presence across Asia Pacific and New Zealand. It will further allow Atos in Australia to diversify its existing industry focus on Maritime, Defence, Defence Industry, Law Enforcement and Government sectors in Australia.
2013	Opmantek	Australian Small Scale Offerings Board	AU$0.7M	Queensland-based IT start-up Opmantek has raised more than $700,000 via the Australian Small Scale Offerings Board, one year after partnering with a Mexican telco giant. Opmantek publishes and licenses network management software.
2013	Anittel Communications Pty Ltd	BigAir Group Limited	AU$7M	BigAir Group Limited has acquired Anittel Communications Pty Ltd, an Australian-based company engaged in offering business communications services including internet and data, voice and video and cloud services.
2013	Readify Pty Ltd	Blue Sky Private Equity Ltd	AU$16M	The management of Readify Pty Ltd, Australia-based software developer, has acquired the company in a management buyout transaction, backed by Blue Sky Private Equity Ltd, the Australia-based private equity firm and a subsidiary of Blue Sky Alternative Investments Limited.

4. Software & information technology

Year	Target	Buyer	Value	Details
2013	InfoMaster Pty Limited	Civica Pty Limited	N/A	Civica Pty Limited a provider of business process services for the public sector, has acquired the local government eServices and planning software business from InfoMaster Pty Limited, specialising in planning and development management software for the local government sector in Australia.
2013	Jedda Systems	Clearswift	N/A	Security firm Clearswift has acquired Australia-based endpoint solutions developer Jedda Systems.
2013	Melbourne IT's Digital Brand Services (DBS)	Corporation Service Company (CSC)	AU$152M	DBS provides online brand protection and consultancy services. CSC hopes to combine the global scale and capabilities of DBS with their own corporate domain and online services.
2013	Quad Solutions Pty Ltd	CountryNet IT Solutions	N/A	CountryNet IT Solutions, an Australia-based software development company has acquired Quad Solutions Pty Ltd, the Australia-based software development company.
2013	XciteLogic Pty Ltd	Datacom Connect	N/A	Datacom Connect, an Australia-based company providing business and technology solutions, has acquired XciteLogic Pty Ltd, an Australia-based ICT consultancy and management company.
2013	Quattro Innovation	Deloitte Australia	N/A	Quattro specialises in Google and Salesforce.com installations. Quattro has been acquired by Deloitte Australia and will add 20 staff to Deloitte's consulting practice.
2013	NXG Business Solutions	Deloitte Australia	N/A	NXG Business Solution specialises in SAP software integration. NXG has been acquired by Deloitte Australia and will add 30 staff to Deloitte's CFO advisory practice.

4. Software & information technology

Year	Target	Buyer	Value	Details
2013	Digicon	Deloitte Australia	N/A	Deloitte Australia has acquired digital consulting firm Digicon, a specialist in website design and web building tools.
2013	The Ma-trixGroup of Companies Pty Ltd	Eka Soft-ware Solu-tions Pvt Ltd	AU$22.08M	Eka Software Solutions Pvt Ltd, the India-based company engaged in providing commodity trading and risk management software, has acquired a significant stake in The MatrixGroup of Companies Pty Ltd, the Australia-based software company that develops state-of-the-art automated commodity handling and management system for the mining and grain industries. The acquisition is in line with Eka Software's growth strategy to provide end-to-end commodity management solutions.
2013	OBS Pty Ltd	Empired Ltd	AU$15M	Empired, an Australia-based information technology services company has acquired OBS, an Aus-tralian company engaged in providing companies with Microsoft technologies for expanding and improving their businesses.
2013	Pacific Micro-marketing Pty Ltd	Experian Plc	US$6.5M	Experian Plc, an Ireland-based company that provides data and analytical tools to organizations and consumers, has acquired Pacific Micromarketing Pty Ltd, which is an Australia-based provider of marketing solutions.
2013	Property Data Solutions (PDS)	Fairfax Me-dia	AU$30M	Fairfax Media has acquired PDS, which is a property research company that provides insights into the Australian property market via its PriceFinder brand to real estate agents, developers and inves-tors.
2013	Connect2Field	Fleetmatics	N/A	Fleetmatics, a global leader in fleet management software, has acquired Connect2Field to further as-sist field service businesses globally to manage, simplify and improve their operations.

4. Software & information technology

Year	Target	Buyer	Value	Details
2013	Zookal	Gemini Israel Venture Funds and Filtro Investments	AU$600K	Zookal, an Australian start-up tertiary education resources sharing and training platform, has raised $600,000 from various investors.
2013	Listech	Hexagon AB	N/A	Hexagon specialises in the provision of design, measurement and visualization solutions and they have acquired Listech, a company that increases the efficiency, accuracy and productivity of professional surveyors and engineers.
2013	White Data Limited	IM Medical Limited	AU$9M	IM Medical Limited has acquired White Data Limited, an Australian-based company engaged in providing disaster recovery and technology solutions management services.
2013	Synovate Aztec Pty Ltd	Information Resources, Inc	N/A	Information Resources, Inc, a US based company engaged in providing marketing and selling services has acquired Synovate Aztex Pty Ltd an Australia-based provider of data information services.
2013	Sensory Networks	Intel	AU$21.5M	Intel has acquired Australia-based company Sensory Networks. Sensory Networks makes pattern matching software designed to speed up finding security vulnerabilities.
2013	Network Neighbourhood	JB Hi-Fi	N/A	JB Hi-Fi has bought a 51 percent stake in Network Neighbourhood, an education focused IT services company, for an undisclosed amount. The deal marks an important step in the expansion of JB Hi-Fi's commercial division, which will now offer professional IT services to businesses across Australia.

4. Software & information technology

Year	Target	Buyer	Value	Details
2013	Praxa Limited	Nexon Asia Pacific	N/A	Nexon provides managed services to the mid-market, originally specialising in telecommunications Nexon now provide more managed services. This acquisition should allow Nexon to offer an end-to-end solution from managing a company's infrastructure right through to implementing their business applications, utilising Praxa's experience in delivering SAP and Microsoft-based solutions.
2013	Scanalyse Holdings Pty Ltd	Outotec	N/A	Outotec has signed an agreement to acquire Scanalyse Holdings Pty Ltd, an Australia-based software technology company with operations in Australia, Brazil, Chile and the United States. Scanalyse provides services in process equipment condition and performance monitoring.
2013	ISS Group Limited	P2ES Holdings, Inc	AU$38M	ISS Group Limited has signed an agreement to be acquired by P2ES Holdings, Inc via a scheme of merger. ISS Group Limited is an Australia-based provider of operational management solutions to oil and gas, minerals, manufacturing and food and beverage industries. P2ES Holdings, Inc is a US-based provider of strategic, financial, and technology services for upstream oil and gas sector companies.
2013	PeoplePoint Software Pty Ltd	Procura	N/A	Procura, a provider of home and community care software in the United States, Canada and Australia, has acquired Australia-based PeoplePoint Software Pty Ltd.
2013	OneShift	Programmed	AU$5M	Programmed has acquired a 27.5% stake in the online recruitment business OneShift.

4. Software & information technology

Year	Target	Buyer	Value	Details
2013	SyncDirect and XPA	Reckon	AU$2M	Reckon has acquired both SyncDirect, which allows the transfer of data from a multitude of accounting systems, and XPA, a report writer for professional accountants.
2013	Adtraction Marketing Limited	ReelTime Media Limited	NZ$1M	ReelTime Media Limited has acquired Adtraction Marketing Limited, a New Zealand-based company that delivers targeted marketing solutions and is also the largest directory agency in New Zealand.
2013	Webster Computer Systems	ReelTime Media Limited	AU$750K	ReelTime Media Limited has acquired Webster Computer Systems, an IT services business that handles OEM specialist products from a range of vendors.
2013	AvPlan	Simon Hackett	AU$1M	Simon Hackett has acquired 40% of AvPlan, an Australian company that develops iPad-based flight planning software for professional pilots.
2013	Gem Accounts	SimPRO Software	AU$1M	SimPRO Software has acquired a 30% stake in Gem Accounts, an accounting software platform.
2013	Birchman Group Asia Pacific Pty Ltd	SMS Management & Technology Limited	AU$25M	SMS Management & Technology Limited has acquired Birchman Asia Pacific an IT solutions provider based in Perth.
2013	Indicium Technology Group Pty Ltd	SMS Management & Technology Limited	AU$22M	SMS Management & Technology Limited, the listed Australia-based company providing consulting, technology and system integration related services, has agreed to acquire Indicium Technology Group Pty Ltd, the Australia-based provider of end-to-end technology services. The acquisition of Indicium will support company's growing managed services and infrastructure consulting capability, and meets the company's strategic imperative to increase its annual revenue.

4. Software & information technology

Year	Target	Buyer	Value	Details
2013	Bravura Solutions Limited	Stockholm Solutions Pty Ltd	AU$56.77M	Stockholm Solutions Pty Ltd has agreed to acquire 35.17% in Bravura Solutions Limited. Stockholm Solutions Pty Ltd, an Australia-based investment holding company having interest in companies providing wealth management applications and professional services.
2013	JCurve	Stratatel Limited	N/A	Stratatel Limited, an Australian software company, has acquired the software design and promotion business of JCurve.
2013	The Nintex Group Pty Ltd	TA Associates Management, LP; Updata Partners	AU$213M	TA Associates Management, LP and Updata Partners, have agreed to acquire an undisclosed stake in Nintex, the Australia-based software and services provider.
2013	Fred IT Group	Telstra	AU$25M	Telstra has acquired a 50% stake in health technology provider Fred IT Group.
2013	DCA Health	Telstra Corporation Limited	AU$40M	Telstra has agreed to purchase DCA Health, an Australia-based company engaged in the development of customer management applications for health organisations.
2013	Kony Solutions	Telstra Ventures	AU$18.3M	Telstra Ventures has acquired a stake in Kony Solutions, as it looks to grow its mobile and multichannel platform. Kony provides a mobile app development platform dubbed KonyOne, which allows for the creation of applications for a range of operating systems and devices.
2013	Park Assist Pty Ltd	TKH Group NV	N/A	TKH Group NV, the listed Netherlands-based supplier of systems and networks in the fields of information and telecommunication technology and in the electrical engineering and industrial sectors, has agreed to acquire Park Assist Pty Ltd, the Australia-based company engaged in offering parking guidance system for managing car parks.

4. Software & information technology

Year	Target	Buyer	Value	Details
2013	White Labelled	UXC Limited	N/A	UXC Limited, Australia-based ICT consultancy firm, has acquired White Labelled, a leading e-commerce solutions provider.
2013	Quantium Group Pty Limited	Woolworths Limited	AU$20M	Woolworths has acquired a 50% non-controlling stake in data-analytics company Quantium.
2013	RosterLive	WorkForce Software Inc	AU$9.95M	WorkForce Software Inc, a US based company, engaged in providing workforce management solutions has acquired RosterLive, an Australia-based company also engaged in providing workforce management solutions.
2012	Distra Pty Ltd	ACI Worldwide, Inc	AU$48.75M	ACI Worldwide, Inc, the US-based provider of enterprise e-payments software and services, has acquired Distra Pty Ltd, the Australia-based company engaged in developing payments applications.
2012	Nexbis Limited	Agathis Capital LP	AU$80M	Nexbis Limited has been acquired by Agathis Capital LP Nexbis Limited is an Australian company engaged in provision of mobile application development consulting services.
2012	Oniqua MRO Analytics	ASCO Group	AU$13.6M	ASCO Group Limited, the UK based company engaged in the provision of supply chain solutions and logistics services, has acquired an 80% stake in Oniqua Pty Ltd., the Australia based company engaged in the provision of asset performance management solutions.
2012	HipChat	Atlassian	N/A	Sydney-based Atlassian Software, a leading provider of collaboration software for product teams, today announced it has acquired San Francisco-based HipChat, a hosted private chat service for companies and teams.

4. Software & information technology

Year	Target	Buyer	Value	Details
2012	BigHand Limited	Bridgepoint Development Capital	AU$80M	BigHand Limited, the Australia based developer of digital dictation software, has been acquired by Bridgepoint Development Capital, the UK based private equity firm.
2012	TransLogix Systems Pty Ltd	CargoWise Pty Limited	N/A	CargoWise Pty Limited, the Australia based company engaged in developing and marketing of logistic management solutions has acquired TransLogix Systems Pty Ltd, the Australia based company engaged in providing transport, freight, logistics, third party logistics and warehouse software solutions.
2012	Assetic Pty Ltd	Carnegie Private Opportunities Fund; Carnegie Venture Capital Fund	AU$10M	Carnegie Venture Capital Fund and Carnegie Private Opportunities Fund have acquired a 55% stake in Assetic Pty Ltd, an Australia based company engaged in design and development of data management solutions. Both Australia based funds are managed by Mark Carnegie who is interested in design and development of data management solutions.
2012	Brand-screen	Co-investors: Macquarie Capital Group Limited; SingTel Innov8 (Singapore) and Southern Cross Venture Partners (Palo Alto and Sydney)	US$11M	Brandscreen announced it is looking to receive further investments. The Series B round was led by Macquarie Capital Group Limited and was joined by new co investors including SingTel Innov8 (Singapore) and existing investor Southern Cross Venture Partners (Palo Alto and Sydney).
2012	Kestral Computing Pty Ltd	Constellation Software Inc/Gary Jonas Consulting	N/A	Gary Jonas Consulting, a wholly owned subsidiary of Constellation Software has acquired Kestral Computing, a software provider to radiology and laboratory information systems in Australia, New Zealand and Asia.
2012	Sonar Limited	Cornerstone OnDemand	AU$14M	Sonar is a leading provider of cloud-based talent management solutions serving small businesses globally.

4. Software & information technology

Year	Target	Buyer	Value	Details
2012	Logro	Deloitte Australia	N/A	Deloitte Consulting has announced it will be joined by the team from SAP BI services firm, Logro.
2012	Apt Business Solutions Pty Ltd	DWS Ltd	AU$5.7M	IT Services firm DWS Ltd has announced that it has signed an Asset Purchase Agreement to acquire the business assets of Canberra-based Apt Business Solutions Pty Ltd (provider of outsourced application managed services to major Federal Government Agencies, including the Defence Force).
2012	TekInsure	eBaoTech	N/A	eBaoTech, a leading software provider for the life and property & casualty insurance industry across Europe, Asia and the Americas, will acquire TekInsure, a Sydney, Australia-based insurance software company.
2012	Fintechnix	Ebix, Inc	N/A	Ebix, Inc, a leading international supplier of on-demand software and e-commerce services to the insurance industry, today announced that its Australian operation has acquired Fintechnix, a leading supplier of web-based straight through processing solutions to the Australian Life Insurance and Wealth Management sectors.
2012	Conducive Pty Ltd	Empired	AU$8M	Empired, a listed Australia-based IT consulting services provider, has agreed to acquire Conducive, which is an Australia-based IT consulting services provider.
2012	COGITA Holdings Limited	Epicor Software Corporation	N/A	Epicor has acquired all of the assets of COGITA Holdings. Epicor Software Corporation is a global leader in business software solutions for manufacturing, distribution, retail and services organizations.

4. Software & information technology

Year	Target	Buyer	Value	Details
2012	IT Domains	Expert Solutions Providers	N/A	Expert Solutions Providers announced its acquisition of IT Domains, an established IT provider and value added reseller within the Microsoft environment.
2012	Salmat Limited	Fujifilm Holdings Corporation	AU$375M	Tokyo's Fujifilm Holdings Corporation has announced that it signed a definitive agreement with Australia's Salmat Limited to acquire Salmat's Business Process Outsourcing division.
2012	Ideas International Limited	Gartner Inc	AU$13M	Gartner Inc has acquired Ideas International Limited. Gartner Inc, a US-based company providing information technology research and advisory services. Ideas International Limited, an Australia-based company, is a supplier of information technology research.
2012	Lan 1 Pty Ltd	Hills Holdings	N/A	Hills Holdings, a listed Australia-based investment company in the electronics and communications business, has acquired Lan 1, an Australia-based company in the business of distribution of internet protocol storage, networking, security and surveillance products.
2012	BearingPoint	HiSoft	N/A	China's biggest provider of outsourcing services, HiSoft, entered the Australian market after buying local consulting firm BearingPoint.
2012	ioGlobal	Imdex Limited	AU$8M	Imdex Limited, a listed Australia-based company engaged in providing drilling fluids and downhole instrumentation to the mining, oil and gas, water well and civil engineering industries, has agreed to acquire ioGlobal which is an Australian-based company engaged in providing innovative cloud-based data management solutions.

4. Software & information technology

Year	Target	Buyer	Value	Details
2012	Lexmark International, Inc	ISYS Search Software	AU$32M	ISYS Software, an Australian global leader in embedded search and universal information access solutions has acquired Lexmark.
2012	Tapit	Jon Medved and other investors	AU$2.4M	Australia's Tapit has raised $2.4 million from investors. Tapit's technology allows individuals to download information and transact by tapping their phones on objects like outdoor advertising, product packaging or shop windows.
2012	Sky Technologies	Kony Solutions	N/A	Melbourne firm Sky Technologies - specialists in mobilising SAP environments - was bought out by US-based mobile platform maker Kony Solutions.
2012	ENGAGE Pty Ltd	LivePerson, Inc	N/A	LivePerson, Inc, a US-based provider of real-time engagement solutions, announced that it has signed a definitive agreement to acquire ENGAGE Pty Ltd, an Australian provider of cloud-based customer contact solutions, established in partnership with the Clemenger Group.
2012	CSG Limited	NEC	AU$227M	NEC will acquire the technology solutions business of Australian ICT firm CSG Limited. The technology solutions business of CSG provides end-to-end IT solutions and services, including managed and enterprise services and strategic consulting.
2012	nMetrics Pty Limited	Net Optics Ltd	N/A	Net Optics, Inc, a US-based software solutions company, has acquired nMetrics, an Australia-based developer and seller of network and performance monitoring and reporting solutions to managed service providers and cloud vendors.

4. Software & information technology

Year	Target	Buyer	Value	Details
2012	nMetrics and Triplelayer	Net Optics, Inc	N/A	US-based Net Optics, Inc, a leading provider of Intelligent Access and Monitoring Architecture solutions, has acquired Sydney-based nMetrics, a network and application analysis software vendor and its sister company, Triplelayer, a private Australia-based distributor.
2012	Innogence	NTT Data Business Solutions Australia Pty Ltd	N/A	NTT Data Business Solutions Australia Pty Ltd, the Australia-based company provider of SAP solutions and services for medium and large organizations, has agreed to acquire Innogence, the Australia-based software development company, for an undisclosed consideration.
2012	Stream Holdings Pty Ltd	Oxygen Business Solutions	N/A	Oxygen Business Solutions, a wholly owned subsidiary of UXC Limited and provider of SAP software and services, has completed an agreement to acquire 100% of the shares of Australian specialist SAP consulting firm, Stream Holdings Pty Ltd.
2012	Stream Technologies	Oxygen Business Solutions Pty Limited	N/A	Oxygen Business Solutions, a NZ based provider of IT and SAP consulting services (subsidiary of Australia-based UXC), has agreed to acquire Stream Technologies, an Australia-based company specialising in SAP ERP and NetWeaver consulting.
2012	ScriptRock	Peter Thiel	AU$1.2M	Peter Thiel, a Facebook board member and PayPal co-founder, has invested $1.2 million in a funding round for business software maker, ScriptRock.
2012	Tripoint Online Pty Ltd	Red Rock Consulting	N/A	UXC Limited has announced that it's wholly owned subsidiary Red Rock Consulting has completed the acquisition of the business of Oracle integrator Tripoint Online Pty Ltd.

4. Software & information technology

Year	Target	Buyer	Value	Details
2012	Jireh Consulting Services Ltd	Red Rock Consulting	N/A	UXC Limited has announced that it's wholly owned subsidiary Red Rock Consulting has completed the acquisition of all the shares of Auckland-based JD Edwards Consulting firm Jireh Consulting Services Ltd.
2012	IMC	Ricoh	N/A	Ricoh Australia has acquired the IT services business of IMC Communications. IMC Communications has been specialising in providing end-to-end IT Infrastructure services. The deal will bolster Ricoh's strategy to be a complete technology services-based organisation.
2012	Coin Software Pty Ltd	Rubik Financial Limited	AU$23.18M	Rubik Financial Limited, the listed Australia-based company, engaged in investing in forestry and other agribusinesses, has acquired Coin Software Pty Ltd, the Australia-based company providing financial planning software.
2012	SolveIT Software	Schneider Electric	N/A	Schneider Electric, a French global specialist in energy management, has signed an agreement to acquire SolveIT Software, an Adelaide -headquartered scientific software provider specialising in supply & demand chain optimisation and predictive modelling.
2012	SolveIT Software	Schneider Electric	N/A	Schneider Electric, a French global specialist in energy management, has signed an agreement to acquire SolveIT Software, an Adelaide-based scientific software provider specialising in supply & demand chain optimisation and predictive modelling.
2012	Atmail	Starfish Ventures	AU$2M	Atmail will accelerate its push into the cloud email space after a $2 million cash injection from local venture capitalist Starfish Ventures. Atmail develops email and web communications software for large companies and telecoms vendors.

4. Software & information technology

Year	Target	Buyer	Value	Details
2012	IPscape	Telstra	AU$5M	Telstra has invested almost $5M in IPscape, a Sydney-based global provider of contact centre applications and technology that enables organisations to transform expensive and complex legacy contact centre setup.
2012	Whispir	Telstra Corporation	AU$4M	Telstra will invest $4 million in funding into Melbourne-based cloud company Whispir.
2012	Learning Seat Pty Limited	The Riverside Company	N/A	The Riverside Company, the US-based private equity firm, has agreed to acquire Learning Seat Pty Limited, the Australia-based developer and provider of e-learning courses.
2012	Consolidated Media Holdings Limited	Twenty-First Century Fox, Inc	AU$2073M	Consolidated Media Holdings Ltd received a binding proposal from News Corporation to acquire all its issued shares.
2012	Maxnet Ltd	Vocus Communications Limited	N/A	Vocus has entered a binding agreement to acquire more than 30% of New Zealand based datacentre operator and cloud provider, Maxnet.
2012	Promax Applications Group	Wipro Limited	AU$35M	Wipro Limited, an IT solutions and services provider, signed an agreement to acquire Promax Applications Group, a leading player in trade promotion planning, management, and optimization solutions.
2012	Max Solutions Holdings Limited	Xero	AU$6M	Xero already owned 15.9% and it has agreed to pay $2 million cash and $4 million of Xero shares for the remaining 84.1%. The shares will vest over three years.

5. US venture capital deals

Year	Target	Investor	Value	Details
2015	Employment Innovations	Partners for Growth	US$4M	Partners for Growth has invested US$4M into Employment Innovations, which provides cloud-based, employment award compliance solutions.
2014	Invoice2Go	Accel Partners	US$35M	Australian start-up Invoice2Go, which provides invoicing solutions, has received a US$35M investment from Accel Partners.
2014	ScriptRock	August Capital, Valar Ventures and others	US$8.7M	ScriptRock is an Australian start-up that primarily provides products that allow companies to adequately determine what IT infrastructure they have and how that infrastructure fits together. ScriptRock has received US$8.7M in funding from several investors including Peter Thiel's Valar Ventures. Peter Thiel was a founding investor in Facebook and Paypal.
2014	BugHerd	Australian based Tank Stream Ventures and Starfish Ventures and US-based 500 Startups	AU$1M	Australian start-up, BugHerd which provides bug tracking and task management software has raised AU$1M from series A shares.
2014	Nitro	Battery Ventures	US$15M	Nitro, an Australian startup that produces software that eliminates the need for printing, scanning and other paper-based processes has secured a US$15M investment from US VC fund Battery Ventures.
2014	Campaign Monitor Pty Ltd	Insight Venture Partners	AU$266M	Insight Venture Partners, a US-based venture capital firm has acquired an undisclosed stake in Campaign Monitor Pty Ltd, an Australian based provider of software solutions for managing email marketing campaigns.
2014	Viocorp	Partners for Growth	N/A	N/A

5. US venture capital

Year	Target	Investor	Value	Details
2014	LIFX	Sequoia Capital	AU$12M	LIFX an Australian start-up that provides multicolour LED 'smartbulbs' that can be controlled by a mobile device has received an investment of AU$12M from US venture capital fund Sequoia Capital.
2014	Canva	Shasta Ventures and Founders Fund	US$3.6M	Canva, Australian online design website, has raised an additional US$3.6M in a second round of funding with an earlier initial round of funding of US$3M coming from Matrix Partners, Blackbird Ventures and Square Peg Capital.
2014	Siteminder	Technology Crossover Ventures	US$30M	Online hotel distribution and connectivity platform, SiteMinder, has raised US$30 million in funding led by Palo Alto-based Technology Crossover Ventures.
2014	Yuruware Pty Limited	Unitrends, Inc and Insight Venture Partners	AU$10M	Unitrends Inc, the US-based provider of data protection appliances and US-based private equity firm Insight Venture Partners have acquired Yuruware Pty Limited, Australian based company developing cloud technologies for migration, monitoring and business continuity for Amazon Web Services and other public cloud systems.
2014	Shoes of Prey	Various investors including Andy Dunn, the co-founder of Bonobos and David Spector, a former Sequoia Capital partner.	US$6.5M	Australian online fashion retailer Shoes of Prey has raised a further US$6.5M in funding in order to fund its push into brick and mortar stores.

5. US venture capital

Year	Target	Investor	Value	Details
2013	Bubble Gum Interactive	Bill Tai and various other investors	AU$2.5M	Games studio Bubble Gum Interactive has raised $2.5 million in a second round of funding. Bubble Gum Interactive is an independent virtual worlds and games studio.
2013	App.io	Quest Venture Partners	US$1M	App.io is a Melbourne-based startup that helps brands promote their apps, find new users and offers tools that allow iOS applications to run in the browser using HTML5 technology.
2013	Bigcommerce	Revolution Growth	US$40M	Bigcommerce was established in 2009 to create software that allows small businesses to create their own online stores. The company has raised US$35M from other US-based venture capitalists.
2013	BuyReply	Valar Ventures, Square Peg Ventures and Adrian MacKenzie	AU$1M	Sydney-based BuyReply, founded by entrepreneur Brad Lindenberg, is a new kind of eCommerce platform that allows offline mediums to become transactional.
2012	Bigcommerce	Mike Maples and General Catalyst Partners	AU$20M	Early Twitter investor Mike Maples has joined US venture capital firm General Catalyst Partners in backing Sydney-based tech start-up Bigcommerce, an e-commerce platform provider, which has secured $20 million in funding.
2012	Happy Inspector	US investors	AU$1M	Happy Inspector, a time-saving iPad app for property inspections, has raised seed funding from US investors, after finding it difficult to raise funds locally.

6. Initial public offerings

Year	Company	Sector	Funds raised	Details
2015	Manalto	Internet	N/A	Following a reverse takeover of Healthlinx in 2013, Manalto a United States based social media software company, is seeking to raise AU$6M in its IPO this year.
2015	Other Levels	Internet	N/A	United States based Other Levels, a company that provides mobile marketing and analytics services are set to launch on the ASX rather than the US markets.
2015	InfoTrack Pty Ltd	Internet	N/A	InfoTrack, a company that allows law firms and conveyancers to search for information on property titles and plans, is planning an IPO for later this year and expecting to raise as much as AU$200M
2015	Touchcorp	Software	N/A	Touchcorp is an Australian digital payments system. The company has been valued at AU$162M and is set to launch on the ASX this year.
2015	Superloop	Telco	N/A	Superloop is set to launch on the ASX and is chasing a AU$17.5M IPO. Superloop is a dark fibre infrastructure provider.
2015	Future Fibre Technologies Pty Ltd	Telco	N/A	Future Fibre Technologies is planning an IPO for later this year. Future Fibre Technologies manufactures and markets fibre optic intrusion detection technologies.
2014	eCargo Holdings Limited	Internet	AU$30M	eCargo Holdings, a Chinese based provider of integrated online and offline supply chain solutions for retail stores, has listed on the ASX.
2014	3P Learning Limited	Internet	AU$337M	3P Learning Limited is the developer of Mathletics, an online mathematics e-learning tool, as well as other e-learning software for children.

6. Initial public offerings

Year	Company	Sector	Funds raised	Details
2014	SurfStitch Group Limited	Internet	AU214M	SurfStitch Group operate a popular online fashion store.
2014	Urbanise.com Limited	Internet	AU$108M	Urbanise.com is the first cloud-based platform designed specifically for delivering services to buildings
2014	Australian Careers Network Limited	Internet	AU$142M	Australian Careers Network Limited is a provider of vocational education and training services
2014	Victor Group Holdings Limited	Media	AU$4M	Victor Group Holdings Limited provides marketing management training, brand planning, marketing strategic planning in Australia.
2014	APN Outdoor Group Limited	Media	AU$424M	APN Outdoor Group is an outdoor advertising company, operating across Australian and New Zealand.
2014	oOh!media Limited	Media	AU$289M	oOh!media Limited is an outdoor advertising company.
2014	LatAm Autos Limited	Media	AU$33M	LatAm Autos is an online classifieds and content platform operating principally in the Latin American automobile industry.
2014	Appen Holdings	Software	AU$15M	Appen, an Australian entity that develops highly specialised data sets that allow machines to learn how to write and read has listed on the ASX.
2014	Citadel Group Limited	Software	AU$46M	Citadel Group, an Australian provider of IT services, has listed on the ASX.
2014	Orion Health Group limited	Software	AU$112M	Orion Health, the eHealth provider, has dual listed on both the Australian and New Zealand stock exchanges.
2014	OneVue Holdings Limited	Software	AU$46M	OneVue provides financial management software platforms and has listed on the ASX at AU$0.32 per share.

6. Initial public offerings

Year	Company	Sector	Funds raised	Details
2014	Bailador Technology Investments Limited	Software/IT	AU$58M	Bailador Technology Investments Limited is an expansion capital investment fund operating in the technology sector.
2014	iSentia Group Limited	Software/IT	AU$408M	iSentia provides media monitoring services across Asia-Pacific.
2014	Gentrack Group Limited	Software/IT	AU$159M	Gentrack develops and implements specialist software for energy utilities, water companies and airports.
2014	Vista Group International Limited	Software/IT	AU$171M	Vista Group provides cinema management software, film distribution software and customer analytics software to companies across the global film industry.
2014	BPS Technology Limited	Software/IT	AU$58M	BPS Technology develops trading and payment platforms for merchants. It also provides cloud-based, software-as-a-service payment systems for both alternative and cash-based economies.
2014	Enverro Ltd	Software/IT	AU$7M	Enverro develops cloud-based workforce management applications.
2014	DTI Group Ltd	Software/IT	AU$25M	Digital Technology International provides advanced surveillance systems and solutions for the global mass transit industry.
2014	Aconex Limited	Software/IT	AU$312M	Aconex develops online document management, web collaboration and project management software for construction, engineering and facility management.
2014	Catapult Group International Ltd	Software/IT	AU$21M	Catapult Group International Ltd is an Australian based company that develops devices for capturing sports analytics.
2014	8common Limited	Software/IT	N/A	8common is a software as a service provider. 8common provides financial and accounting software services.

6. Initial public offerings

Year	Company	Sector	Funds raised	Details
2014	Aeeris	Software/IT	AU$6M	Aeeris, the emergency warning provider, is seeking to raise AU$6M in its initial public offering.
2014	BPS Technology	Software/IT	AU$28M	BPSTechnology, the Australian provider of trade exchange management systems and mobile payment platforms, is set to list on the Australian Securities Exchange with 28 million shares being sold at AU$1 each.
2014	Rewardle Holdings	Software/IT	AU$4M	Rewardle, an Australian digital coffee card provider, is set to make an initial public offering price of 20c a share for 20 million shares with the aim of raising AU$4M.
2014	SpeedCast International Limited	Telco	AU$235M	SpeedCast is a global network and satellite telecommunications service provider.
2013	PS&C	Internet	AU$25M	PS&C, a corporate IT services provider, opened December 2 at $1 issue price but closed at $0.89 on its debut.
2013	Ozforex Group	Internet	AU$439.4M	OzForex, which provides online payment services in more than 50 currencies, opened October 11 at $2 issue price and closed on the first day at $2.56.
2013	iSelect	Internet	AU$215.3M	iSelect, an online insurance comparison company, opened June 24 at $1.85 issue price, but closed on its first day of trading at $1.56.
2013	Nine Entertainment Co Holdings	Media	AU$624.6M	Nine Entertainment opened December 6 at $2.02 issue price but closed at $1.98.
2013	Freelancer	Telco	AU$15M	Freelancer, an outsourcing website, opened November 15 at $0.50 issue price and closed at $1.60 on its first day of trading.

7. Back door listings

Year	Company	Sector	Funds raised	Details
2015	Norwood Systems Limited	Software/IT	N/A	Norwood Systems, a phone technology systems company is looking to list on the ASX following a reverse takeover of failed mining group Monteray.
2015	AHAlife	Internet	N/A	AHAlife is set to list on the ASX following the announcement of a 100% takeover of ASX listed shell company INT Corporation. AHAlife is a high-end online US designer marketplace.
2015	Animoca Brands Corporation	Internet	N/A	Animoca Brands Corporation, a developer of mobile games, has listed on the ASX following a reverse takeover of Black Fire Minerals Ltd.
2015	Brainchip	Software/IT	N/A	Brainchip, which provides neural computing technology, is set to list on the ASX following a reverse takeover of Aziana.
2015	DirectMoney	Internet	N/A	DirectMoney is set to list on the ASX following a reverse takeover of Basper, a former automotive parts distributor. DirectMoney is a non-bank money lender.
2015	Dubber Corporation Limited	Software/IT	N/A	Dubber Corporation, an entity that provides call recording services, is set to list on the ASX following a reverse takeover of Crucible Gold Limited.
2015	iSignthis	Internet	N/A	iSignthis, an identity verification and online signing service provider, has listed on the ASX following a reverse takeover of Otis Energy.
2015	Rision	Internet	N/A	Rision, an online recruitment service provider, is set to list on the ASX following a reverse takeover of Reclaim Industries.
2015	Spookfish Limited	Software/IT	N/A	Spookfish, which provides geospatial imaging products, has listed on the ASX following a reverse takeover of White Star Resources Limited

7. Back door listings

Year	Company	Sector	Funds raised	Details
2015	Tomizone	Internet	N/A	Tomizone, a New Zealand based entity that provides Wi-Fi connections, has listed on the ASX following a reverse takeover of PHW Consolidated.
2015	Yatango	Software/IT	N/A	Yatango is set to make its debut on the ASX following a reverse takeover of Latitude Consolidated Limited.
2014	1-page	Internet	N/A	1-page, a US based cloud HR services provider, is doing a reverse takeover of ASX listed InterMet Resources.
2014	Big Review TV	Internet	N/A	Big Review TV is set to launch on the ASX following its reverse takeover of Republic Gold. Big Review TV is a video based review web site.
2014	Bulletproof Group Limited	Internet	N/A	Bulletproof Limited, a cloud services provider, is set to list on the ASX following a reverse takeover of Spencer Resources Limited.
2014	Cloud Central	Internet	N/A	Cloud platform provider Cloud Central has integrated with wine company Dromana Estate to list on the ASX.
2014	Cocoon Data	Internet	N/A	Information security company Cocoon Data has listed on the ASX by using uranium explorer Prime Minerals the company now trades as Covata.
2014	Collaborate Corporation Limited	Software/IT	N/A	Collaborate Corporation, a developer of peer-to-peer networks, has listed on the ASX following a reverse takeover of Qanda Technology Limited
2014	Connexion Media Limited	Internet	N/A	Connexion Media Limited, a cloud services provider, has listed on the ASX following a reverse takeover of ECSI Limited.

7. Back door listings

Year	Company	Sector	Funds raised	Details
2014	Crowd Mobile	Software/IT	N/A	Crowd Mobile has been acquired by Q Limited in a backdoor listing. Crowd Mobile provides mobile entertainment.
2014	Decimal Networks	Internet	N/A	Decimal Networks, a cloud financial planner, has listed on the ASX using mineral exploration company Aviva Corporation.
2014	digitalBTC	Internet	N/A	digitalBTC, Australia's first online bitcoin exchange has listed on the ASX using a company known as Macro Energy.
2014	Ensogo Limited	Internet	N/A	Ensogo Limited, an online shopping website, has listed on the ASX following a reverse takeover of iBuy Group Limited.
2014	Fatfish Internet Group Limited	Telco	N/A	Fatfish, a Singaporean internet venture accelerator, has listed on the ASX following a reverse takeover by Atech Holdings.
2014	Grays Online	Internet	N/A	Grays Online have combined with Mnemon, the combined group to be known as Grays eCommerce Group. The combined group will be the largest listed e-commerce group in Australia.
2014	iCollege Limited	Internet	N/A	iCollege Pty Ltd, an online education provider, has listed on the ASX following a reverse takeover by DGI Holdings Limited.
2014	iSentric	Internet	N/A	iSentric a mobile banking platform and mobile payments service provider has listed on the ASX following a reverse takeover of SE Asian Digital Commerce & Media.
2014	iWebGate Limited	Internet	N/A	Provider of virtualisation technology, iWebGate has listed on the ASX following a backdoor takeover by MyATM Holdings Limited.

7. Back door listings

Year	Company	Sector	Funds raised	Details
2014	Mig33	Software	N/A	Mig33 will be bought by Latin Gold, in a deal which will see the company renamed as MigMe.
2014	Montech Holdings Limited	Internet	N/A	Montech, a cloud services provider, is set to list on the ASX following a reverse takeover of Sirius Corporation Limited.
2014	Mpire Media	Media	N/A	Mpire has launched on the ASX following a reverse takeover of Lithex Resources.
2014	NewZulu	Internet	N/A	PieNetworks acquired crowd-sourced journalism site Newzulu to bolster its ASX standing.
2014	Primary Opinion Limited	Internet	N/A	Primary Opinion, an online legal services provider, is set to list on the ASX following a reverse takeover of Jumbuck Entertainment Limited.
2014	PRM Clouds	Internet	N/A	Cloud applications builder has joined with miner Minerals Corporation to list on the ASX.
2014	Rhype Limited	Software/IT	N/A	NewLease Pty Ltd has listed through a backdoor listing with FRR Corporation Limited with the combined entity renamed to Rhype Limited.
2014	SkyFii	Internet	N/A	SkyFii is set to launch on the ASX after a reverse takeover deal was struck with RKS Consolidated, a former investment company. SkyFii provides free WiFi in retail stores in exchange for customer's shopping habits.
2014	Spring.Me	Internet	N/A	Australian based social network Sping.Me has listed on the ASX through a reverse takeover of resources firm GRP Corporation
2014	Stream Group	Software/IT	N/A	Stream Group has listed on the ASX following a backdoor listing through a shell company. Stream Group provides claim processing software.

7. Back door listings

Year	Company	Sector	Funds raised	Details
2014	XTD Limited	Media	N/A	XTD Limited, a digital advertising provider, has listed on the ASX following a reverse takeover of White Eagle Resources Limited.
2014	XTV Networks Limited	Internet	N/A	XTV Networks, an online video service provider, has listed on the ASX following a reverse takeover of Intercept Minerals Ltd.
2014	YPB Group	Software/IT	N/A	YPB Group, a Chinese-based developer of applications to identify forgeries, has listed on the ASX following a reverse takeover of Australia Mining Company.
2014	ZipTel	Telco	AU$200K	ZipTel, an Australian based company that offers cheap pre-paid SIM cards for phone and internet users that travel abroad, has listed on the ASX using a shell company known as Skywards.
2013	Applabs Technologies Ltd	Software/IT	N/A	Applabs, which is a mobile application developer, has listed on the ASX following a reverse takeover of AACL Holdings Limited.
2013	Disruptive Investment Group	Internet	N/A	Disruptive Investment Group, a developer of retail, franchise and e-commerce brands, has listed on the ASX following a reverse takeover of Allied Consolidated Limited.
2013	Shoply Limited	Internet	N/A	Shoply, an online shopping website, has listed on the ASX following a reverse takeover of Adeffective Limited.
2013	TTG Fintech Limited	Internet	N/A	TTG Fintech, which provides transaction authentication services, has listed on the ASX following a reverse takeover of TTG Mobile Coupon Services.

This list in this chapter is owned by Norton Rose Fulbright and licensed to the author for the purposes of this book.

CHAPTER 7

About the Author

Nick is deeply involved in the Australian technology, media
and telecommunications (TMT) sector as a lawyer, non-
executive director, angel investor, speaker and former Dot-
com entrepreneur.

Nick is a corporate lawyer with a focus on TMT. He has a
detailed understanding of digital technology & media
businesses – from a commercial as well as legal viewpoint. He
has worked on over $3 billion of TMT-related transactions
since 2012, including a number of the M&A/investment
transactions mentioned in this book. He also regularly advises

on tech procurements, cloud, privacy, cyber-risk and e-business matters.

Nick is the leader of Norton Rose Fulbright's APAC Communications, Media & Technology Group and was Head of Sydney Office for 5 years. Norton Rose Fulbright is the world's fifth largest law firm. Nick's group has won the *Australian Technology Law Firm of the Year Award* and Nick has been identified as a leading lawyer in his field in numerous directories, including *Chambers, Asia Pacific Legal 500* and *Best Lawyers.*

Digital disruption is an area of special interest for Nick. Not only does he advise some of Australia's largest companies on the legal aspects of the issue, he is an investor in successful online legal disruptor, www.lawpath.com. Nick writes regularly on technology and disruption for the *Australian Financial Review,* the *Sydney Morning Herald* and *The Age* newspapers.

His unique expertise in the TMT field was gained through hands-on industry experience with major law firms in Australia and Tokyo as well as being a Chief Operating Officer with listed Dot-com group, Spike Networks in Los Angeles, during 2000-2002 (and part of the team that listed Spike on the ASX, raising $35 Million).

Prior to Spike, Nick was a Creative Executive with John Wells Productions, on the lot at Warner Brothers in Los Angeles. In this role, Nick worked on the development and production of the TV shows, *ER & The West Wing,* and fifteen feature firm projects. Nick secured his role with Warner Brothers as a result of having completed a Masters of Film & TV Producing at the University of Southern California.

Currently, Nick is a Non-executive Director of ASX-listed software company, Integrated Research (IRI:ASX). He is a Governor of the American Chamber of Commerce. Nick is a

past President of the Australian Communications and Media
Law Association. He is on the Federal Government's
Consultative Working Group on Cyber Safety and the NSW
Government's Procurement Advisory Board. He is a director
of the Institute for Economics & Peace (ranked in the top 15
Most Impactful Think Tanks in the World with revenues < $5
million pa). Nick is a member of the Australian Institute of
Company Directors.

He has started and exited several businesses. In 1996, he
founded the *Tokyo Comedy Store* and was the hosting comic for
several years before selling the business which is still
operating today. He was the lead writer/actor in the Japanese
TV show *The Ugly Gaijin Brothers.* He produced the
mockumentary *Searching for Alison Porchnik* featuring Woody
Allen, Debra Messing, Willie Nelson & Carol Kane.

Nick speaks at over 40 events each year on subjects such as:
- Your Company & Disruption: How you can use
  disruptive forces to create a better company
- Your Career & Disruption: How you can use
  disruptive forces to create the career you want
- How to Understand & Manage Cyber-risk
- Structuring Successful Tech Mergers & Acquisitions
- Big Data & the Internet of Things

Please feel free to contact Nick at newpathleaders@gmail.com
Follow Nick on Twitter @NickAbrahams

CHAPTER 8

Stay Up-to-date with Disruption & Special Offers

To receive regular updates on deal activity and to find out more about disruption and courses designed to help entrepreneurs, investors and corporates successfully embrace disruption, please join the New Path Leaders mailing list by sending an email to newpathleaders@gmail.com

If you have an idea for a business but you are struggling to get traction (or even started), try Pollenizer's 60-day Entrepreneur Course [www.pollenizer.com/60-day-startup/]. Readers get 25% off the standard price, paying just $150 (ex GST) by using this promo code DISR.

Index

121cast, 120
1337 Ventures, 75
1Form Online Pty Ltd, 96
1-page, 56, 154
25Fifteen, 79
3P Learning Limited, 149
4impact Group Pty Ltd, 124
5th Finger, 67, 120
8Common Limited, 125, 151
96FM, 112
99designs, 39, 62, 68
AAPT, 58, 108
Accel - KKR, 77
Accel Partners, 13, 39, 43, 63, 68,
    77, 146
Accenture Plc, 112
ACI Worldwide, Inc, 138
Aconex Limited, 151
ACP Magazines Ltd, 117
Acquire Learning Pty Ltd, 88
Active Display Group, 114
Acumen Ventures Adelaide, 75
aCure Technology Pty Ltd, 106
Adage, 88
Adam Internet, 58, 67, 95, 102
Adam lockers, 102
Adconion Pty Limited, 112
Adelaide Angel Investors, 76
AdNear, 39, 92
Adslot Limited, 94
Adtraction Marketing, 136
Adtraction Marketing Limited,
    136
Adventure Capital, 74
Aeeris, 152
Aegis Media Australia, 114
AFC Group Pty Ltd, 103

Affinity Equity Partners, 111
AFL Telecommunications LLC,
    103
Agile Sports Technologies, Inc,
    123
AHAlife, 153
Airbnb, 7, 18, 21, 52
Airtasker, 7, 8, 20, 36, 53, 86, 89
AirTree Ventures, 14, 35, 74, 86,
    87, 89
Alibaba, 16, 57
All Homes Pty Ltd, 93
Allegro Networks, 98
Allegro Private Equity, 119
Alphabird, 115, 117
Amaysim, 56
Amazon, 11, 12, 21, 147
Amblique Pty Ltd, 122
Amcom, 34, 79, 103, 104, 106
America Fujikura Ltd, 106
Amobee, 68, 112, 121
AMP, 17
AMP Ventures, 17, 74
AMT Group, 109
Analytics Group, 38, 127
Angel Cube, 78
Animoca Brands Corporation,
    153
Anittel, 33, 128, 131
Ansible Mobile Pty Limited, 107
Anywhere Healthcare, 89
ANZ, 17, 78
ANZ InnovyzSTART, 78
APN, 54, 65, 66, 97, 98, 112, 115,
    120, 150
App.io, 148
Appen Holdings, 150

Applabs Technologies Ltd, 157
Applaud IT, 103
Apple, 6, 16, 20, 117
Apt Business Solutions Pty Ltd, 140
Ardent Ventures, 75
Arnold Travel Technology Pty Limited, 88
Arte Mobile Technology, 113
Artesian Venture Partners, 17, 74
Arunta Resources Limited, 103
ASCO Group, 138
Ascom Holding AG, 131
ASG, 34, 131
Asia Principal Capital, 72
Assetic Pty Ltd, 139
Atlassian, 13, 14, 18, 35, 39, 43, 45, 52, 57, 61, 62, 68, 69, 86, 99, 126, 138
Atmail, 144
Atomic Sky, 78
Atos SE, 131
ATP Innovations, 78, 80
Audio Network, 112
Audio Products Group, 128
August Capital, 77, 146
Aura Capital, 98
Aurelius Digital, 76
AussieCommerce, 41, 54, 89
Austar United Communications, 118
Australasian Wealth Investments Limited, 113
Australian Associated Press Pty Ltd, 117
Australian Association of Angel Investors, 76
Australian Careers Network Limited, 150

Australian Independent Business Media, 120, 122
Australian Investment Network, 76
Australian Local Search Pty Ltd, 116
Australian Satellite Communications, 110
AutoBase Limited, 102
Aviva Corporation, 55, 155
AvPlan, 136
AWI Ventures, 79
Bailador, 35, 74, 98, 151
Banijay Entertainment SAS, 117
Battery Ventures, 77, 146
Bauer Media, 111, 117
BearingPoint, 67, 141
Beautyheaven Group, 111
Belgiovane Williams Mackay Pty Ltd, 111, 121
Best Recipes, 96, 100
Betfair, 36, 89
Betteroff Networks Pty ltd, 104
Beyond International Ltd, 117
Big Review TV, 154
BigAir, 33, 58, 98, 103, 107, 126, 131
Bigcommerce, 39, 59, 61, 62, 68, 69, 93, 148
BigHand Limited, 139
biNu, 110
Birchman Group Asia Pacific Pty Ltd, 136
Bitcoin, 16, 22, 35, 41
Blackbird, 14, 35, 74, 147
Blacksheep Capital, 74
Blinkbox Music, 90
Blue Chilli, 78, 92, 130
Blue Sky Ventures, 74, 131
BlueChilli, 35
BlueHill Asset Management, 75

Booz & Co, 60
Box, 17, 60, 97, 99, 102
BPS Technology, 151, 152
Brainchip, 153
Brand New Media Pty Ltd, 115
Brandscreen, 139
brandsExclusive, 54, 65, 89, 98
Brasil Online and OCC, 101
Bravura Solutions Limited, 137
Bridgepoint Development
   Capital, 139
Brisbane Angels, 76
Brisbane Technology Park, 78
Bubble Gum Interactive, 148
Buchanan Group Pty Ltd, 122
BugHerd, 39, 146
Bulletproof Group, 55, 154
Bullseye, 92
Business Access Group, 126
Business Aspect Group, 38
Business Records Management
   LLC, 129
Business Spectator Group, 8
Buspak Advertising (Hong
   Kong) Limited, 112
Buyinvite, 65, 100
BuzzNumbers, 121
C3, 125
C4i Pty Ltd, 109
Call Plus, 103
Callafin, 72
Campaign Monitor, 8, 13, 39,
   43, 44, 52, 53, 146
Canberra Data Centres, 34, 129
Cannings/Cannings Purple, 118
Canon, 126
Canva, 39, 147
Careerone Pty Limited, 88
CargoWise Pty Limited, 139
carsales.com.au, 5, 37, 54, 63, 88,
   89, 95

Carthona Capital, 74
Catalyst Investment Managers
   Pty Ltd, 118
Catapult Sports, 126, 128, 151
CatchOfTheDay, 58, 65, 69, 98,
   99
Celfino Ltd, 75
Centre for Organisational
   Innovation, 125
Centurion Investments Services
   Pty Ltd, 113
CharterNet, 81
Chomp, 117
Citadel Group Limited, 124, 150
Citigroup, 71
Citrix Ventures, 74
Civica Pty Limited, 132
Clearswift, 132
Click PR, 83
Clipp, 123
Clive Mayhew, 88
Cloud Central, 56, 154
Cloud9 Software, 40, 93
CLSA/Citic, 72
CMB Captial, 72
Cocoon Data, 55, 154
Codan Limited, 109
COGITA Holdings Limited, 140
Cognizant Technology Solutions
   Corporation, 126
Coin Software Pty Ltd, 144
Collaborate Corporation
   Limited, 154
Collins Collective, 80
Commonwealth Bank, 17, 125
Communications Australia Pty
   Limited, 108
Computers Networks Pty
   Limited, 130
Conducive Pty Ltd, 140
Connect2Field, 53, 59, 133

Connexion Media Limited, 154
Consolidated Media Holdings
    Limited, 145
Constellation Software Inc, 139
Convergence Ventures, 75
ConvertU2 Technologies and
    CU2 Global, 128
COO, 68
Cornerstone OnDemand, 139
Corporation Service Company,
    132
Costa Group, 41
CountryNet IT Solutions, 132
CPI International Holding Corp,
    109
Creative Enterprise Fund, 76
Creative Industries Innovation
    Centre, 78
Credit Suisse Emerging Markets,
    71
Credit Suisse Investments
    (Australia) Limited, 118
Crowd Mobile, 155
Crowe Horwarth, 82
Crown Castle Australia, 103, 109
Crown Resorts, 36, 89
CSG, 67, 142
Cuscal, 37, 89, 126
Dailydo, 89
Data#3, 38, 126, 127
Datacom, 127, 132
Dataweave, 124
DCA Health, 137
Deals.com.au, 100
DealsDirect, 59, 96
Decimal Networks, 55, 155
DecTech, 37, 55, 127
Delivery Hero Holding, 100
Delling Advisory, 72
Deloitte, 38, 59, 61, 71, 82, 124,
    127, 132, 133, 140

Dentsu Aegis Network Limited,
    111
Depo8, 80
Desktop Mapping Systems Pty
    Ltd, 124
Dicker Data, 127
Digicon, 60, 133
Digital 4ge, 78
Digital CC, 55
Digital Performance Group Ltd,
    118
digitalBTC, 55, 155
Dimension Data, 38, 127
Dimmi, 67, 87, 102
DirectMoney, 153
Discovery Technology, 38, 127
Disruptive Investment Group,
    90, 157
Distra Pty Ltd, 138
Divvy, 130
DMG Radio Australia Pty Ltd,
    119
Doctape, 126
DocuSign, 17, 39, 93
Dodo, 58, 107
Domain Group, 93
Dr Foster, 125
Dragonrider Opportunity Fund
    II LP, 118
Dromana Estate, 56, 154
Dropbox, 52, 97
DTDigital Pty Limited, 100
DTI Group Ltd, 151
Dubber Corporation Limited,
    153
DWS Advanced Business
    Solutions Limited, 124
DWS Ltd, 140
East Ventures, 75
Eatability Pty Limited, 100
EatNow, 65, 98

eBaoTech, 140
eBay, 20
Ebix, Inc, 140
Ebook Library, 96
eBUS Limited, 116
eCargo Holdings Limited, 149
EDC, 34
Edge Loyalty Systems, 122
Edrolo, 86
Eftel, 58, 66, 107, 109
Eka Software Solutions Pvt Ltd, 133
Elemental, 93
Ellerston Capital, 36, 65, 90, 99
Empired, 133, 140
Employment Innovations, 146
Enepath, 123
ENGAGE Pty Ltd, 142
Engin Pty Limited, 109
Ensogo Limited, 155
Enterprise Data Corp, 104
Enverro Ltd, 151
Enzumo Group of Companies, 127
Eon Broadcasting Pty Ltd, 115
Epicor Software Corporation, 140
Equity Venture Partners, 36, 94
Ernst and Young, 71, 125
Eskander's Betstar, 36, 55, 91
Euler Capital LLC, 86
Exelis Inc, 109
Expedia, 20, 36, 39, 52, 90
Experian Plc, 133
Expert Solutions Providers, 141
Expert360, 9
Express Data, 127
Eye Corp Pty Ltd, 120
Ezi Holdings Pty Ltd, 127
Ezidebit, 37

Facebook, 39, 52, 63, 64, 143, 146
Facilitate Digital Holdings Limited, 94
Fairfax, 36, 53, 66, 92, 93, 95, 98, 111, 114, 115, 118, 133
Fairfax Radio Network Pty Ltd, 114
Fantero, 36, 54, 90
Fatfish Internet Group Limited, 155
Federation Capital, 72
Fenox Venture Capital, 75
Festvue Inc, 99
Filtro Investments, 134
Finite, 82
FinTech, 9, 16, 17
Fintechnix, 140
First Point Global, 125
Fishburners, 80
Fitbit, 6
Fitlink, 92
Fleetmatics, 59, 133
Fort Street Advisers, 71
Forum Media Group GmbH, 115
Founder Institute, 74
Founders Fund, 39, 77, 147
Foxconn, 56
Foxtel, 118, 119
Fred IT, 60, 137
Freelancer, 8, 36, 54, 60, 62, 90, 152
Friedman Corporation, 124
Friendorse, 97
Frontier Accelerator, 75
FujiFilm Holdings, 67, 141
Funtastic Limited (Madman group companies), 114
Future Capital Development Fund, 99

Future Fibre Technologies, 41,
    149
FX Networks, 106
Ganji.com, 100
Gartner Inc, 141
GB Group, 37, 55, 127
GBS Ventures, 74
Gem Accounts, 136
Gemini Israel Venture Funds,
    134
General Catalyst Partners, 77,
    148
Gentrack Group Limited, 151
GEON Group, 119
Glentel Inc, 109
Global Payments Inc, 127
Global syndicate, 99
Global Television Limited, 116
Globecast Australia, 111
goCatch, 37, 59, 94, 95
GoConnect Limited, 113
Gold Coast Innovation Centre,
    78
Golden Gate Ventures, 75
Goldman Sachs, 72
Goldminex Resources Limited,
    127
Google, 6, 16, 18, 21, 68, 110,
    132
GP Sports, 126
GrabOne, 66, 97
Gracenote, Inc, 113
Grant Samuel, 72
Grant Thorton, 82
Grays Online, 49, 58, 95, 155
GREE Ventures, 75
Green Lane Digital, 74
Griffin Accelerator, 79
GRP Corporation, 56, 156
Guvera, 90
Hall, 72, 82, 86

Happy Inspector, 68, 148
Harbour IT, 126
HarveyNash, 82
HBO, 57
HealthEngine, 60, 97
Henly Club, 80
Hexagon AB, 134
Hi-5 Operations Pty Limited,
    118
HighPoint Capital Pty Ltd, 115
Hills Holdings, 69, 104, 115, 128,
    141
HiPages, 8, 36, 90
HipChat, 138
HiSoft, 67, 141
HomeAway, 36, 95
Hoyts, 111, 113, 121
Human Edge, 38, 55, 130
HWW Ltd, 113
Hyro Limited, 119
iBoss, 104, 106
iCar Asia, 95
iCareHealth, 40, 93
ICE Systems, 125
iCentral, 80
iCollege Limited, 155
ID Leisure International Capital,
    113
IdeaObject, 130
Ideas International Limited, 141
Ignition Labs, 78
iiNet, 33, 34, 58, 66, 68, 95, 104,
    109
iLab, 78
Illuminate Capital, 72
Illyria Pty Ltd, 119
ILX Group Plc, 107
IM Medical Limited, 134
IMC, 144
Imdex Limited, 141

Imorial.com and EventArc.com, 99

Impact Ventures, 75

Inabox Group, 33, 128

Inanda Partners, 73

iNC Digital Media, 115

Independent Media Distribution Plc, 116

Indicium Technology Group Pty Ltd, 136

Indigenous Business Australia, 110

Infinitive, 37, 54, 129

Infitecs Pty Ltd, 124

InfoMaster Pty Limited, 132

Infoplex Pty Ltd, 108

Information Resources, Inc, 134

InfoTrack, 41, 149

ingogo, 37, 41, 56, 59, 87, 97

Innergi, 123

Innogence, 143

Innov8, 17, 67, 139

Innovation Bay, 76, 77

Innovation Centre, 78

Innovyz, 17

Insight Venture Partners, 13, 38, 39, 43, 52, 77, 146, 147

Insight4 Pty Ltd, 129

Inspire9, 80

Integrated Wireless Pty Ltd, 131

Integrators Breeze and Technology Effect, 128

Intel, 17, 59, 74, 134

Intelligent IP, 58, 107

Inteq, 73

Interact Learning Pty Ltd, 96

InterMet Resources, 56, 154

Internode, 66, 109

Intrepica, 92

Investors' Organisation, 76

Invigor Group Limited, 90

Invitetobuy.dk, 91

Invoice2go, 8, 13, 42, 43, 44, 146

ioGlobal, 141

IP Health, 60

Ipera Communications, 110

iProperty, 36, 92

IPscape, 67, 145

IPSTAR Australia Pty Ltd, 104

Iress Limited, 123

Iron Mountain Incorporated, 123

iSelect, 60, 152

iSentia Group Limited, 151

iSentric, 113, 155

iSignthis, 153

ISS Group, 59, 135

ISYS Search Software, 142

IT Domains, 141

iWebGate Limited, 155

j2 Global, 91, 104

Jacanda, 73

JB Hi-Fi, 134

JCurve, 137

Jedda Systems, 132

Jireh Consulting Services Ltd, 144

Jolimont Capital, 74

JP Morgan, 65, 72, 99

Jump On It, 100

Jungle Capital, 74

Just Eat, 9, 87

Kestral Computing Pty Ltd, 139

Kickstart Ventures, 75

KidSpot, 8

KIT Digital, Inc, 119

Kite Ventures, 100

KK Fund, 75

Kloud Solutions, 125

Knowledge Partners Pty Ltd, 125

Kodak, 35

Kohlberg Kravis Roberts & Co
  LP, 119
Kondoot, 101
Konica Minolta Business
  Solutions Australia Pty Ltd,
  125
Kony Solutions, 60, 137, 142
KPMG, 17, 72, 91, 125
KTM Capital, 73, 90
Ladbrokes, 36, 55, 91
Lagardere Unlimited Australia
  Pty Ltd, 119
Lan 1 Pty Ltd, 141
LatAm Autos Limited, 150
Latin Gold, 49, 56, 156
LawPath, 9, 19
Leadtec, 38, 130
Learning Seat Pty Limited, 145
Leon Serry, 91
Lexmark International, Inc, 142
Liberty Financial, 86
Life.SREDA VC, 75
LIFX, 39, 147
Lightspeed Ventures, 77
LinkedIn, 64
Listech, 134
Live Nation, 119
LivePerson, Inc, 142
Living Social, 100
Logro, 140
LoveByte, 91
LP, 137, 138
M.H. Carnegie & Co, 74
M2, 58, 66, 68, 103, 107, 110
Macquarie Group, 59, 72, 74,
  100, 139
Macquarie Radio Network
  Limited, 114
Macquarie Telecom, 103
Macro Energy, 55, 155

Madman Film and Media Pty
  Ltd, 114
Magicseaweed Ltd and Rolling
  Youth Press Pty Ltd, 87
Majoran Distillery, 80
Malaysia Venture Capital
  Management, 76
Manalto, 149
Mandalay Digital Group, Inc,
  107
Manly Emporium, 80
Mannagum Capital, 73
Marketplacer, 123
Markitforce, 122
Martin Jetpack, 41
Match Media, 111
MatrixGroup of Companies Pty
  Ltd, 133
Matrixx, 105
Maverick Marketing and
  Communications, 122
Max Solutions Holdings
  Limited, 145
Maxnet Ltd, 145
Media & Capital Partners, 83
Medinexus, 93
MediNexus, 40
Megabus Pty Ltd, 124
Megaport, 104
Melbourne Angels, 76, 128
Melbourne IT, 53, 87, 88, 91,
  132
Menulog, 87
MenuLog, 9
Merkle, 67, 120
Merlon Health Communications
  Pty Ltd, 115
Message Stick Communications
  Pty Ltd, 110
Metaverse Makeovers, 128

Metro Media Publishing, 111, 118

Metronode Pty Ltd, 108

Mi9, 111

mia Pty Ltd, 107

Microsoft, 38, 68, 100, 116, 129, 133, 135, 141

Mig33, 49, 56, 156

Mirin Capital, 76

Mitchell Lake, 82

Mnemon, 49, 59, 96, 155

Mnet Group Limited, 107

Mobile Embrace, 114, 123

MOKO Social Media Limited, 91

Monk's Hill Ventures, 76

Montech Holdings, 124, 128, 156

Moore Stephens, 73, 82

Morning Crest Captial, 86

Morph Ventures, 76

Morrison Media, 114

Motopia Limited, 128

Moula Money, 86

Mpire Media, 156

Munro family, 59, 96

Muru - D, 78

My strata Pty Ltd, 126

MyNetFone, 103, 104, 108

MYOB, 41, 97

MySale Group, 91

MyTeamDeals, 98

Nabo, 94

National Roads and Motorists Association, 86

Navman, 6

NBN Co, 32, 33, 39, 105

NEC, 67, 108, 142

Nectar Partners, 73

Nemco, 105

Neon Stingray, 38, 130

Neopost SA, 88

NEP, 114, 116

Net Optics, 142, 143

Neto E-commerce Solutions Pty Ltd, 123

NetRegistry, 53, 91

Netus, 115

Network Neighbourhood, 134

Network Ten Pty Ltd, 120

New Ventures Institute at Flinders University, 78

Newport Capital, 73

News Limited, 96, 100, 116, 120

NewSat, 103

Newzulu, 50, 56, 156

Nexbis Limited, 138

Nexon Asia Pacific, 135

Nextec, 73

Nextgen, 58, 68, 108

nextmedia Pty Ltd, 115

Nimble, 41

Nine Group, 57, 66, 92, 101, 102, 111, 114, 116, 152

Nine Live, 111

Ninemsn Pty Limited, 116

Nintex, 59, 61, 137

Nintex Group, 137

Nitro, 146

nMetrics, 142, 143

Norwood Systems Limited, 153

NSC Group Pty Ltd, 108

NSI Ventures, 76

nSynergy, 129

NTT Data Business Solutions Australia Pty Ltd, 143

NXG Business Solutions, 60, 132

O2 Networks, 33, 55, 106

Oakton, 38, 127

Oasis Active, 53, 92

OBS Pty Ltd, 133

OCC Mundial, 86, 87

Occasional Butler, 36, 53, 89

Oceanic Broadband, 105
Oddfellows Pty Ltd, 114
Odecee, 38, 126
Ogilvy, 92, 100
One Africa Media, 116
One Ventures, 14, 74
Oneflare, 8,, 36, 88, 94
OneShift, 36, 88, 92, 135
OneVue Holdings Limited, 150
Oniqua MRO Analytics, 138
Ontario Teachers' Fund, 58, 108
oo.com.au, 95
oOh!media Limited, 150
Ooyala, 67, 102
Open Universities Australia, 96
OpenLearning, 88
Opmantek, 131
Optimal Cable Services Pty Ltd,
    106
Optus, 17, 32, 66, 67, 68, 100,
    105, 110
Optus-Innov8, 74, 76, 120
Oriel Technologies, 33, 126
Orion Health Group, 40, 93, 150
Orion Satellite Systems Pty
    Limited, 104
Other Levels, 149
Ouffer.com, 100
Outdoor Media Operations Pty
    Limited, 120
Outotec, 135
Outware Mobile, 87
Overture Capital, 73
Oxygen Business Solutions, 143
Oyala, 17
Ozefax Pty Limited, 104
Ozforex, 39, 62, 152
OzForex, 43, 60, 68, 152
Ozforex Group, 152
OzSale, 58, 65
Ozsale.com.au, 100

P2ES, 59, 135
Pacific Micromarketing Pty Ltd,
    133
Pacific Star Network Limited,
    114
Pacnet, 33, 105
Pactel International Pty Ltd, 110
Pandora, 64
Panviva, 39, 93
Park Assist Pty Ltd, 137
Partners for Growth, 39, 52, 77,
    146
Pawshake, 89
PayPal, 63, 143
Pedestrian Group Pty Ltd, 111
PennyTel and iVoiSys, 108
PeoplePoint Software Pty Ltd,
    135
Performance Factory, 114
Pier Capital, 73
Pinion, 68, 100
Pixable, 68, 121
PJA Solutions Pty Ltd, 124
Platinum Equity, LLC, 105
Pollenizer, 79, 161
Posse, 92
Pottinger, 73
PR Group, 83
Praxa Limited, 135
Premium Movie Partnership,
    119
Primary Opinion Limited, 156
Prime Minerals, 55, 154
Primus, 66, 110
Primus Telecom Australia, 110
PRM Clouds, 56, 156
Procura, 135
Professional Performance
    System Pty Ltd, 90
Proficeo Ventures, 76
Progility Pty Ltd, 107

Programmed, 36, 92, 135
Promax Applications, 67, 145
Property Data Solutions (PDS),
 133
ProQuest LLC, 96
PS&C, 38, 60, 128, 152
PT Telekomunikasi Indonesia
 Tbk, 105
Publicis Groupe SA, 111
Pure Hacking, 38, 128
Purple Communications, 118
PushStart, 79
PWC, 60
Q Ltd, 117
Q&A social network, 56
Qanda Webspy Business, 99
Quad Solutions Pty Ltd, 132
Quadrant Private Equity, 34,
 120, 129
Quantium, 60, 61, 138
Quattro Innovation, 60, 132
Queens Collective, 80
Quest Venture Partners, 77, 148
Questek Australia Pty Ltd, 104
Quikflix, 57, 99, 114
QUT Creative Enterprise
 Australia, 79
Rampersand, 74, 96
RateSetter, 88
REA Group, 5, 36, 63, 92, 96,
 101
Reactive Media, 112
Readify Pty Ltd, 131
Recall Holdings Limited, 123,
 129
Reckon, 136
Record Point, 73
Recruit Loop, 82
Red Bubble, 101
Red Rock Consulting, 143, 144
Redbubble Ltd, 87

Reed Business Information, 118
Reeltime Media, 92, 136
Reinventure, 17, 35, 54, 74, 94
Revolution Growth, 59, 77, 148
Revolver Creative, 80
Rewardle Holdings, 152
Rhype Limited, 129, 156
Ricoh, 144
Right Click Capital, 74
Ripple, 17, 42
Rision, 153
RiverPitch Brisbane, 77
Riverside Partners, 67
Riverside Ventures, 74
Rocket Internet, 54, 65
RosterLive, 138
RSVP, 36, 53, 92
Rubik, 37, 54, 129, 144
RXP Services, 38, 129
RXP Services Limited, 129
Salmat, 67, 141
Saltbrush Group, 38, 130
Scale Investors, 74
Scanalyse Holdings Pty Ltd, 135
Scancorp, 73
Schneider Electric, 144
Screentime Pty Ltd, 117
ScriptRock, 39, 143, 146
Search Results Group, 90
SEEK, 5, 14, 86, 87, 101, 116
SeekAsia Limited, 86
Sendle.com, 86
Sensis, 54, 105, 116
Sensory Networks, 59, 134
Sentia Media, 117, 121
Sequoia Capital, 39, 77, 147
Serko Limited, 88
ServiceSeeking, 8
Seven West Media, 60, 68, 94,
 97
SFX Entertainment Inc, 117

Shasta Ventures, 77, 147
Shenzhen Infinova, 38, 130
ShineWing Australia, 73
ShippingEasy, 65, 101
Shoes of Prey, 39, 65, 99, 147
Shoply Limited, 157
Sierra Ventures, 77
Silk Studios, 114
Simile Venture Partners, 76
SimPRO Software, 136
Singapore Telecommunications, 121
SiteMinder, 39, 43, 52, 98, 147
Sketchbook Ventures, 74
Sky Network Television Limited, 118
Sky Technologies, 142
SkyFii, 34, 156
Slingshot Jumpstart, 80
Slush, 77
SmartWard, 127
SMP Security, 33
SMS Management & Technology Limited, 136
SNP, 55, 106
SocietyOne, 54, 94
SolveIT Software, 144
Sonar Limited, 139
Sony Pictures, 38
Southern Cross Telco Pty Ltd, 110
Southern Cross Venture Partners, 75, 139
Spaze Ventures Pte Ltd, 76
Spectrum Equity, 77
SpeedCast, 34, 103, 105, 110, 152
Spencer Resources, 55, 154
Spidersat Communications, 67
Spirit Telecom (Australia) Pty Ltd, 103

Spookfish Limited, 153
Sports Marketing & Management Pty Ltd, 119
Sportstec Limited, 123
Spreets group, 12
Spring.me, 56, 156
Springboard Enterprises Australia, 80, 81
SPS Commerce, 38, 130
Square Peg, 14, 35, 37, 39, 75, 94, 147, 148
SR7, 91
Starfish Ventures, 75, 101, 102, 144, 146
Stargate, 37, 54, 129
Start Nest, 80
StartHere, 98
Startmate, 79
Startup Tasmania, 79
Stayz, 36, 95
Stockholm Solutions Pty Ltd, 137
Stone and Chalk, 81
Stratatel Limited, 137
Strategic Payments Services, 37, 89, 126
Strategy Group, 94
Stratton, 37, 54, 89
Stream Group, 156
Stream Technologies, 143
StudioCanal SA, 121
STW Communications, 114, 121, 122
Styletread, 59, 65, 96, 101, 102
SunHotels Group, 94
Sunshine Coast Broadcasters Pty Ltd, 115
Superloop, 149
Surfdome.com, 92
SurfStitch, 61, 87, 89, 92, 150

Swann Communications, 38, 130
Switched on Media, 121, 122
Sydney Angels, 76
Sydney Capital Partners, 73
Sydney Seed Fund, 36, 75, 94
SydStart, 77
Symplicit Pty Ltd, 124
SyncDirect and XPA, 136
Synovate Aztec Pty Ltd, 134
TA Associates, 59, 137
Tagroom.com, 91
Tank Stream Labs, 81
Tapit, 142
Target, 38
Taskbox, 36
Teamsquare, 81
Tech2 Group, 33, 104
Tech23, 77
Technology Crossover
    Ventures, 39, 43, 52, 77, 147
Technology Effect and Breeze, 124
Technology One Limited, 124
TekInsure, 140
Telcom New Zealand
    International, 103
Telekom Indonesia, 33
TeleSign, 33, 55, 106
Telstra, 6, 7, 9, 17, 20, 32, 33, 34,
    39, 40, 41, 54, 56, 58, 60, 63,
    67, 68, 75, 89, 92, 93, 97, 102,
    105, 106, 108, 110, 111, 123,
    125, 130, 137, 145
TelstraClear Ltd, 110
Temando, 65, 88, 99, 102
TenCent, 57
The Cluster, 81
The Iconic, 58, 65, 69, 99
The Intelligent Investor
    Publishing Pty Ltd, 113

TidyMe, 9, 87
Tiger Pistol, 96
Time Telecom, 66, 110
TKH Group NV, 137
TMT Partners, 73
TNF Ventures, 76
Tom Waterhouse NT Pty Ltd, 97
Tomizone, 154
Torque Data, 123
Totem Industries Pty Ltd, 117
Totem Onelove Group Pty Ltd, 117
Touchcorp, 41, 149
TPG, 58, 68, 108
TR Hirecom, 108
Trade Me, 66, 98, 102
TransLogix Systems Pty Ltd, 139
Tribal Group Plc, 130
Trinity Opportunities Limited, 122
TripAdvisor, 36, 55, 87, 94
Tripalocal, 86
Tripoint Online Pty Ltd, 143
TTG Fintech Limited, 157
Twenty-First Century Fox, Inc, 122, 145
Twitter, 64, 97, 148, 160
TYME (Take Your Money
    Everywhere), 125
Uber, 7, 18, 21, 37, 52, 59
UberGlobal, 88, 97
UBS, 72, 97, 98
UniSuper, 103
Updata Partners, 137
Urbanise.com Limited, 126, 150
UXC, 130, 138, 143, 144
Valar Ventures, 77, 146, 148
Valtech, 38, 130
Vector Capital, 44, 78
Venture Advisory, 73

Venture Incubator Space, 79
VentureCrowd, 75, 87
Venuemob, 120
Verde Group, 82
Viatek Services Pty Ltd, 130
Viator, 36, 55, 94
Vibewire, 81
Vickers Venture Partners, 76
Victor Group Holdings Limited,
    150
ViDM Pty Ltd, 117
Village Roadshow, 48, 67, 122
Vinomofo, 99
Viocorp, 39, 52, 146
Virgin Australia Group, 123
Vista Group International
    Limited, 151
Viva9 Pty Ltd, 118
Vividwireless Group Ltd, 110
Vocus, 34, 48, 103, 104, 106,
    110, 131, 145
Vodafone New Zealand, 110
Volt Media, 115
WA Angel Investors, 76
Wanda Cinema Line, 111
We Are Hunted, 97
Web24 Group Pty Ltd, 91
Webjet, 94
Webster Computer Systems, 136
WeightWatchers, 6
Wesfarmers, 17
Western Technology
    Investments, 78

Westpac, 17, 54, 94
Whispir, 145
White Data Limited, 134
White Labelled, 138
Wholesale Investor, 75
Wikidocs, 126
William Hill Plc, 97
WIN Corporation Pty Ltd
    (Adelaide television station),
    116
WindowLogic, 131
Wipro, 67, 145
Wisetech, 41
Woolworths, 60, 61, 138
WorkForce Software Inc, 138
Wotif, 21, 36, 90
XciteLogic Pty Ltd, 132
Xero, 19, 53, 63, 145
XTD Limited, 157
XTV Networks Limited, 157
Yahoo!7, 12
Yarra Capital Partners, 75
Yatango, 56, 154
Yelp, 64
York Butter Factory, 79, 81
YPB Group, 157
Yuruware, 39, 52, 147
Yuruware Pty Limited, 147
zeebox Ltd, 120
ZipTel, 157
Zookal, 134

Disclaimer

No warranties

The information in this book are provided "as is" without any representations or warranties, express or implied. The Author makes no representations or warranties in relation to the information and materials provided in this book.

Without prejudice to the generality of the foregoing paragraph,
The Author does not warrant that:

- the information in this book is complete, true, accurate or non-misleading
- nothing in this book constitutes, or is meant to constitute, advice of any kind.

Limitations of liability

The Author will not be liable to you (whether under the law of contact, the law of torts or otherwise) in relation to the contents of, or use of, or otherwise in connection with, this book:

- for any direct loss;
- for any indirect, special or consequential loss; or

for any business losses, loss of revenue, income, profits or anticipated savings, loss of contracts or business relationships, loss of reputation or goodwill, or loss or corruption of information or data.

.

www.ingramcontent.com/pod-product-compliance
Lightning Source LLC
Chambersburg PA
CBHW060026210326
41520CB00009B/1017